REMINISCENCES OF STANLEY H. KRYSZEK

BY

JEAN KRYSZEK CHARD

To order additional copies of this book, contact:
Xlibris Corporation
1-888-795-4274
www.Xlibris.com
Orders@Xlibris.com
39994

CONTENTS

CHAPTER ONE: WARSAW 7

CHAPTER TWO: FRANCE 12

CHAPTER THREE: SCOTLAND 17

CHAPTER FOUR: MIDDLE EAST 22

CHAPTER FIVE: EGYPT 27

CHAPTER SIX: ITALY 32

CHAPTER SEVEN: BRITAIN 42

CHAPTER EIGHT: SOUTH AFRICA 50

CHAPTER NINE: MALAWI 60

POST SCRIPT 67

AFTERWORD 69

Stanley, mid 1970's

CHAPTER ONE

WARSAW

I was born in 1917 in a place called Tomaszow Mazowiecki in central Poland. In those days it was under German occupation, so it wasn't really Poland and became Poland about a year later. My grandfather was Hermann Kryszek. My father, Jakub, was the eldest of thirteen children. He married Bronislawa Zylber. I had a sister, Marja. A brother died in infancy.

My earliest memories of childhood are those of a rather unpleasant brat. I was very naughty, and my jokes weren't very funny at all. Apparently, I was not a particularly endearing child. At the age of about five, I used to hide under the dining room table and pinch people's legs with sugar tongs. Later, little pranks like turning off the light at the switch during dinner parties were commonplace. My parents, at that time, were reasonably well off and I was getting an awful lot of very elaborate toys, if you can say that any toys were elaborate at the age of five, a lot of toy soldiers, which were the standard fare for boys, while the girls were being given dolls.

We lived in Tomaszow until I was two, when my parents moved to Warsaw, where I lived until the outbreak of World War II. I was a precocious little blighter, and learned to read at the early age of three or four years. I could write in printed characters between four and five, and also knew the clock. I entered the elementary school at the age of seven, and after some trepidation and struggles, kept going up, and graduated from high school in 1934. Later that year, I entered Warsaw University and studied medicine for the next five years, until the war broke out.

My general education was fairly good, even though I had been doing my best not to get it, and I just got by. I had some funny brushes with the law and with the professors. Through all this, my mother was a tower of strength because, through thick and thin, she managed to feed and clothe us.

My mother was rather full of life. She was a handsome woman, and quite a hard worker. In those days there was no such thing as a washing machine, or a dishwasher, or an air conditioner, or anything like that. Vacuum cleaners were considered to be a great luxury. She was a good cook, and after my father died of a heart attack, she carried on with the business. I helped her a little, in so far as the medical school permitted, and we made out, somehow. My father had his first heart attack in 1935, then he got better and, against the doctor's advice, he started working, as usual, very hard, and he had the second attack and died in 1936.

My mother was a great cook, and I remember her sour grass soup, or sorrel soup, which I just loved, and never managed to duplicate, simply because I didn't have sorrel. I tried to emulate some of her dishes, and found it very difficult, but I did cook pork and sauerkraut, red cabbage, and all kinds of little meat dishes like cabbage rolls and tomato soup. Also, cutlets and various chicken dishes, macaroni—made at home of course—macaroni and cheese was very good: macaroni with green cheese and sugar and cinnamon. I remember, particularly, the beautiful crêpes my mother made, filled with jam, or blueberries, or just a little cream cheese, cinnamon and sugar. It was really quite delicious.

I think I was about six or seven, and I used to go to parties, children's parties, sometimes at my friend Irene's house. Once, I met a girl was about my height, with long hair, very nicely dressed, and announced I was going to marry her. Well, it didn't work out, somehow. Then, as I started growing up, I had quite a good time, both at school and then at college. I went to a private school, as there were few state schools at that time in Poland. My sister eventually was admitted to one, but that was after I had completed my high school education. It was great fun, going out in Warsaw, and walking through the park, walking through what they called *allées*, long, long, large boulevards. Very, very nice, particularly in the springtime.

I spent most of my early summers in Tomaszow, where my paternal grandfather was a textile manufacturer. In those days, he was well off, and had three horses. One was for a buggy, and two were for coaches. There was a coachman, and it all went on beautifully until the Depression hit, and there were no more coaches and buggies and we had to live much more modestly. However, my visits with my grandparents were always very pleasant.

My grandmother was a great storyteller. She could invent stories about anything, particularly about children's adventures in the woods, her favorite subject. She was a very, very, dear soul. Incidentally, the Germans shot her in Tomaszow. I spent most of my summers with my grandparents, and in addition to that, we made a few trips to other places. One or two to resorts in Poland, to so-called spas, and one or two in Germany, East Germany. I remember well all the experiences.

I enjoyed traveling on the Polish trains, which were quite fast and well equipped and they all carried dining cars. The company was *Wagons Lits et le Grand Express Européen*, and it was a real treat. The service in the dining car was terrific, and the food super. I really enjoyed my time. I was always given one dinner in the dining car when we traveled that way. It was always pleasant. We often went through Warsaw, a beautiful city with parks and gardens.

A particularly interesting part was the Lazienki Palace, which was built by a Polish prince, who was a close relative to the last Polish king, Stanislaw August Poniatowski. That little palace, which was built around 1800, was a very beautiful place, with a park and a lake, with lots of swans, and you could ride on a coach or a jitney all the way around the park. It was quite large, and very well preserved. I believe it's still there, and has not been destroyed, even though the city itself was. There was also a famous castle called Wawel, also a very beautiful ancient relic.

Warsaw became the capital of Poland in the 1600's. Before that, Krakow was the capital, which was much older. Unfortunately, Poland was generally either defending itself or attacking somebody, and it wasn't all that much fun. It would make for a pretty hard history course to try to figure it all out.

My father was a very hard-working man who lived for his family. I remember him taking me out to a café, which I believe existed until the war, called Kleschch. I used to get ice cream, and he had a tall *mazagran*, a dark, sweet drink with a little rum in it. He was fairly well off until the Depression—that was 1929—and it was much harder afterwards until he died almost ten years later. In view of what happened in Poland over the ensuing years, he may have been lucky.

Of course, we had a maid. In fact, practically everybody, rich or poor, who had any kind of family, had a maid, simply because there were absolutely no appliances or kitchen aids. It was impossible to maintain any kind of comfort and establishment without the help. First, when we were better off, we had three maids, afterwards, we had two, and then just one. Those girls were usually from rural areas, where cash came very hard, and they wanted to save up a little money. They were given a room with washbasin and a bathroom, and they had use of the bathtub or shower. They worked two weeks with two days off each time, so they could go home. Very often, they came from a fairly distant location, and they just stayed with friends on their time off. It was a tough life, but so it was for everybody else, and there was no other employment. The country was very poor and, in fact, a lot of those girls wanted to find work of any kind. Fortunately, we had some very nice girls who, even after they left or got married, came back on an odd Sunday just to see us and have a little chat. My mother did an awful lot to make it a close family, and we were, for as long as it lasted.

Eventually—I suppose I was about sixteen, which wasn't at any particularly early age—I started dating. Of course, dating with no money was rather difficult; we didn't have any money, so the thing was to go out for a little ice cream or maybe a glass of hot, black tea with a little sugar. That was what we could afford, once in a while. Of course, there was no television, so people were reading books, and you could always get a cheap movie. Some prime features were rerun immediately in the cheaper theaters, so we used to go and watch the movies, some of them, of course, still silent movies. It's quite interesting to compare what was going on then, afterwards, and now.

Eventually I applied for medical school in Warsaw. At that time, at the age of sixteen, I was very interested in a young lady, and she was living in another city. I had the idea that if I didn't get my admittance to a medical school in Warsaw, I would go to the other town, which was Wilno, and be in the same place where this young lady was. However,

I did get admitted to the Warsaw medical school, and that was when the romance ended. I enjoyed my school days, and I enjoyed the city of Warsaw very much.

At school, we studied up to two o'clock in the afternoon, and then, of course, there was quite a large amount of homework, a lot of reading. As an example, we had to read and review all the Aeschylus, Euripides and Sophocles tragedies. Also, Aristophanes' comedies. We had to study Latin for eight years, which I think was very helpful as far as languages are concerned; a lot of the roots of our European languages come from Latin. I had a friend, with whom I spent a lot of time, just walking in the evenings and talking about things. Those were very, very interesting days, because I was probably better equipped intellectually then than I am now. Oh, that poor soul is gone now.

We played a lot of bridge, and used to go at night to a place called The Horseshoe, a kind of bar, where you could buy a half-portion of fish salad, bread and one large vodka for about eighty cents. That was our big treat after those long, rather cold talks, on which we spent so much time. So I struggled through school, and somehow managed to get by with very good marks. I suppose I was a better cheater than everybody else was.

Student ID 1939

When I started going to the medical school, of course, a completely new life opened up. We were given a little more freedom than high school, and as long as you completed your courses you were all right and they didn't bother you much. Once a week we went to a soccer game; we had two or three good soccer teams, and that was all very exciting. There was quite a lot of social life—on the cheap—usually little student parties, and school and class dances. However, I also managed to get some opera, drama and music.

I loved opera. My first opera was *Lohengrin*. I was eleven years old, and I was wearing short pants. I got a ticket through the school, at a very low price, and sat in the second row, which was just about the most expensive seats in the house. That was my first opera, and I got hooked on it and, particularly, on Wagner, probably simply because that was my first time. One of them was a naughty one, *Orpheus in the Underworld*, with complete ballet. Warsaw opera was good; so was the drama. I saw *Ivan the Great*, and spent a lot of my pennies on quite a number of plays.

And so we arrived close to the war. In the meantime though, I had a very beautiful last two years, from my point of view, because I was at college. I was really growing up, and I was meeting good friends and enjoying life, even though it was on the cheap. We had some great parties; I met some nice girls and boys, and I eventually got engaged, after having broken several hearts.

In 1938, I met a very delightful girl, a member of my youth organization. Her name was Irina Bibiulska. We became very fond of each other. She also liked my family, and my family liked her. We spent a lot of time together, and we had one ten-day vacation on the Polish seacoast in a place called Jastarnia. Irina was quite intelligent, and a very fine girl. When we were on the coast, during the vacation, telegrams started coming from various people to return to Warsaw because the situation was getting very physical. After the Russians and the Nazis made a pact—the so-called Non-Aggression Treaty, which was in fact at that time an alliance—we all knew that war would be inevitable, and quiet mobilization started in Poland.

I remember traveling back on the train from Jastarnia to Warsaw. Irina and I had crossed the city of Gdansk to the train, and though it was a free city it was completely Nazified. We could see German artillery and troops all over the place. That was probably the last train to leave. We got to Warsaw, and a couple days later the war started by unannounced German bombing attacks on Warsaw and other cities. The two of us were glad for those ten days together. We had decided that we intended to get married, but we couldn't consummate the marriage because of the war, so we said good-bye on the second week of the Polish war.

Irina helped my family quite a bit. She was killed fighting the Germans in the Warsaw Uprising in 1944. I heard about that from one of my relatives. So our idea of meeting in Warsaw after the war did not materialize.

It was very sad saying good-bye to my mother and sister. My sister was then at the senior high of a state school, and my mother said, after I had taken them both to a friend's, she said she knew she would never see us three together again. And that is how it went.

Bronislawa (Zylber) Kryszek and Marja Kryszek

CHAPTER TWO

FRANCE

The German blitzkrieg just rolled through Poland. I eventually got hooked up to a unit, about the 6th of September 1939, said good-bye to my family, and started out. I went with a friend from college, another medical student. I also took a cousin of mine, a friend of his, and we started out. We began in the evening, and went marching, marching, marching.

One of the younger fellows was given a flask of brandy by his solicitous mother, who was very worried that he might get cold, or something. After walking all night, he said he had to have a drink. I said, "Well, just look for some water." He said, "No, I think I'm going to have some brandy." And I said, "Don't!" But he did, and he couldn't walk anymore after that. It was just the wrong thing to do. Under the circumstances, we just couldn't take him. So we left him in a little resort near Warsaw, and a young friend, who was with him, decided he was too going to stay. Myself, and the other medical friend, whose name was Nofer, we kept going.

We had the good fortune of seeing an ambulance, which was stopped. In that ambulance was an officer who was one of our school instructors at the medical school, and we asked him if he could take us. So onto the bumpers we jumped, and that's how we traveled. However, after some little distance, there was an air raid, and all available space was given over to the wounded. Off we got, and started walking again. Then we were lucky enough to jump a truck, a flat truck, and we rolled a little further along. After that, we started walking some more. And we walked, and we walked, until we started falling asleep, still walking.

We eventually arrived at a place called Lublin, about 50 miles southeast of Warsaw. It was quite a good-sized city, and there was a university there. We were so tired when we arrived, we were sitting in a cafe, and I couldn't even lift my feet, I had to pick up my leg to cross it. We had coffee and doughnuts, and then there was a big air raid. Everybody was trying to get out of the city center, and they were running out. A lot of people were wounded and killed, and my friend, Nofer, and I became separated, and never got together again.

I found a medical unit and was given marching orders a good distance east. We traveled on one of the few trains still operating to a hospital in eastern Poland, in a place called Rudna. In Rudna, there was quite a bit of confusion, and there was no room for us, so we were sent down to southeastern Poland, and we went by horse and buggy.

We went some distance, and the next day, early in the morning, we got on a train in southeastern Poland. The train rolled very irregularly, moving along, but when it stopped, one of the officers went out to find out what was going on. He came right back, and just said a few words: "They sold us. There is a partition." The Soviets had come in with their army from the east. We got off the train, discussed the situation for a while, and then, when we saw some of the Russians, we decided to evacuate and go to Rumania.

The trip through eastern Poland was very sad, but very interesting. The horses and buggies we traveled on were called *podwodi*; small, suitable for about four people, with a pair of horses and no springs, rather bumpy. In one place, we stopped at a farmhouse, and bought some food, which was cooked by the woman of the house, consisting of very fat pork, and eggs. I developed the worst diarrhea of my life, and for a while it looked as though they would have to leave me, which of course, would mean being taken prisoner. However, I got better, and managed to continue.

After a while, the decision was made by the commander of another train, a hospital train, to go to Rumania. So we went to Rumania. We crossed the border at a place called Lalesczicki, and became refugees a few miles beyond the border.

It was very pleasant, to begin with. The people were very kind, and gave us sausage and grapes. Then back on the train, we traveled bit by bit into Rumania. We stopped at a place called Focsani, a small Rumanian town, very, very, friendly, and we were having coffee my first taste of Turkish coffee—in a little café, and there was an air raid warning. We immediately dropped down on the floor. It was funny because we were so trained by German air raids in Poland that a mock air raid produced the same reaction.

We stayed in Focsani for a day-and-a-half, and then the train took us on, and eventually, after a few days, we reached a place called Braila, which was on the River Danube, the Danube Delta. We were figuring on getting to Turkey.

Much as we were depressed at the news that Poland had only spontaneous resistance in several places, that Warsaw was bombarded daily, and the rest of the country was overrun, we decided we had to go fight somewhere. We planned to go to Turkey from Braila, which was a port on the Black Sea. However, just about that time, a company boat, a company ship of Bayer's, a German pharmaceuticals, arrived in Braila, and for some reason, we were immediately transshipped from there to Constança, still in Rumania, and from there we had no way to Turkey.

We were all arrested and interned, and marched into a camp. The official of the camp, a man called Sindic, gave us the account of where we were going to live, what we were going to do, and what exercises we were going to do. He also said we had to be careful, because there were infectious diseases, and he expected us to have typhoid and a few other diseases.

There were four of us who, after listening to that speech, just walked out of the camp. We found a young Rumanian, who kept us in his house after he bought some civilian clothes for everybody, and after he got us organized we walked to the railway station and got some tickets. However, we didn't want to sit in the station and get caught, so we waited until the train started outside the station towards Bucharest, and we jumped the train. With the tickets, once we were on, we were all right. Of course, we did not have any documentation. I had my student's card; some of the others had documents, some didn't.

After arriving in Bucharest we stayed in a little hotel in two bedrooms. In the middle of the night, we were searched; they were looking for weapons, but we didn't have any weapons. Though we weren't thrown in the clink, we had to sit on the check a while. When they let us out a little later next morning we went to the Polish embassy, which was still operating in Bucharest.

Officially, there was a state of war in Poland, not a total occupation, so we went to the Polish embassy and got ourselves Polish passports, of sorts. We were also given a small amount of money. We then, after we went and got French visas at the French embassy, started for the trains again. However, we couldn't go right away, because only selected people were allowed to get out. Of our group of four, two others were selected first and, about two days later, we got on the train in Bucharest. The man I was travelling with was Kasimir Feinberg, who was at that time a pharmacist, an army lieutenant, and a Polish automobile champion in the sports car category. Of the other two, I met one of them as a medical officer in Northern Rhodesia after the war, when I was in Bechuanaland.

We traveled from Bucharest to Zagreb, in Yugoslavia, which was a very beautiful city full of lovely old architecture, and eventually Feinberg and I reached Italy. There we slept overnight, and got on the Italian train, which was a very good fast electric train, particularly distinguished by large numbers of *carbinieri* watching everybody in the place. There was one *carbiniere* at each entrance and exit. Then, we got to a place called Ventimiglia, which was really in Italy, on the French border. We slept there, and then we started on the French train.

It was a very fascinating journey, right across the French Riviera, with all the beautiful palm trees, and generally gorgeous views. We went through the Italian Riviera and then the French Riviera, and the first, the Italian Riviera, is much more beautiful, while the French Riviera, was much wilder. We stopped at Cannes, where Feinberg had a sister-in-law. Cannes was everything the movies are made of, quite beautiful. We went through Monte Carlo, and kept right on going until we arrived at Paris.

In Paris, we separated. First, we were put in barracks. Then Feinberg went to a military officers' camp, and I, not having had any official military status at the time, was placed in a *Bienvenue des Jeunes Gens Catholiques*, which was a Catholic students' home. It was quite nice there. At least it was a clean room, and a very pleasant concierge who let me in and out.

During that time, I walked a lot through Paris, probably about 10, 15 miles a day, as they used to say, *"per pedes apostolore"*, which is, in translation, "by Apostolic feet". I went to various places like Montmartre and Montparnasse; the Louvre was closed, so I could not go to the Louvre, but the sights in Paris were very interesting, such as Place des Invalides, Place de la Concorde, Arche de Triomphe. I had a little bit of money, and I met a friend who used to live in Poland, but was then living in France. He was married to a French girl in Paris, and we went out together a few times.

The food was very good, and the champagne cheap. But all the time, at the back of my mind, there was the worry about what was going on at home, and the constant news of the bombing of Warsaw. The peninsula of Hel, which was just a small peninsula on the Baltic Sea, where the Polish destroyers were based, was the last point of organized resistance when Warsaw finally fell. This was about the 6th or 8th of October, 1939.

I finally got my marching orders and got on a train. After about half a day, we arrived at an infantry cadet school in a place called Guer. It was a pretty rough place, cold and dirty, and the food was terrible. Guer was very small, and all the people who were quartered there were billeted in private quarters, but the private quarters were rather primitive, and generally consisted of attics. We still had a little bit of money left, so we rented a room for five. At least it was a little bit warmer, because the cold in Brittany was intense. For heating, we used what they called *breuse*, which you could buy for a few centimes per packet, and which was really burned-out charcoal. It glowed, and kept the room warm.

Unfortunately, we eventually ran out of money. The situation in the official quarters was terrible, and the attic was so cold there we had to put everything on before going to bed, including even our backpacks. We had to climb up a ladder to go to bed, and to get out to go anywhere. Eventually, we became very, very miserable. However, I was in the infantry officers' school, and when they asked for candidates for artillery, a lot of us wrote the examination, which was mostly mathematics and physics, and I, having had nothing to do with mathematics and very little to do with physics for five years, decided I was going to write it—and a miracle happened—I passed.

From Guer, we marched to a place called Kroëtkedar, some distance away. It was a larger training base, with various units, some assistants and some help with the horses. It had, most importantly, a clean barrack room with big pots of steaming coffee. After our experiences in Guer, we almost cried to see that. The next day the training started.

We got very good training, but the equipment we were using was strictly World War I vintage. In fact, I had great worries about the French equipment and the quality of the French soldiers. They seemed mainly to drink wine in great *bidons*, walk around with coats unbuttoned, didn't salute, and in general, did not appear as a well-disciplined army. Having seen some of the Germans, I was wondering whether we were ever really going to get out of there.

Kroëtkedar was a typical army base in Brittany, with little hedges and various maneuvering equipment. Twice a week, for a day, we got some artillery equipment training by riding the World War I horse guns and firing at the odd bush or hole in the ground. At night, we studied ballistics, physics, mathematics and tactics.

It really wasn't too bad, considering that we got reasonable food and the munificent sum of 50 centimes a day, which translated to, I think, half a penny. Later on, I was promoted, and got 75 centimes a day. During the course of this training, I got a few days' leave, and went to Paris to see Uncle Henry, who was there. At that time, he was working as a doctor in the Polish clinic in Paris. Also, I met Irene Koprowska, with Claude, who was just a small baby, and Hilary's father, who was also in France. Hilary at that time was, I think, in Rome. It was quite fun to see Uncle Henry and, of course, Cousin Stanley, who was Henry's brother; also, Edda and Tuna were there. We spent a little time together, and after a few days, having commiserated with ourselves, I returned to camp.

Training was fairly intensive, but we couldn't see much in the way of equipment, and we were not excited by the quality of the French troops in that area. Just as the school was graduated, we received the news that the Germans had attacked Belgium and that the Polish troops fighting in Norway were evacuated. Things in France went really bad, from bad to worse. The whole Battle of France took about fourteen days, and the Battle of Dunkirk, even less. The German attack started on the Low Countries, on Belgium, on the 10th of May 1940, and the whole Battle of France was over by July 14.

The Germans literally rolled across France, with no resistance. The only battle where the French troops distinguished themselves was Dunkirk, when they assisted with the evacuation of the British expeditionary force. For all practical purposes, the Battle of France was ended and Paris was occupied on June 14, and organized resistance ceased in France on June 24.

CHAPTER THREE

SCOTLAND

We tried to get to our division, but it was no longer in existence, and as the whole country was cut up we decided we were going to go to England, a long way off. Our group consisted at that time of 49 officers and men. We wanted to take some trucks, which were just standing there, but the French wouldn't let us have them. At gunpoint, we took them anyway, and got out of there. We started going southwest and passed through Bordeaux, which at that time was the seat of what remained of the French government. A very beautiful city, and they still had a lot of very good wine. In a place called Rochambeau, just driving through, I saw the most beautiful woman I have ever seen; I only saw her for about two seconds, but she was very striking.

France was indeed defeated. Nobody wanted to resist. The country was finished. We kept going through northwestern France, through the Bordeaux area, and eventually we reached Bayonne, on the French border, and already expecting to be taken by the Germans. We had a few brushes with the Germans, but they were mostly light motorized elements, and they didn't particularly bother with unorganized units.

In Bayonne, there was a complete confusion. Everybody was trying to get away, somehow. Our major, who was a very enterprising man, arranged with the captain of a French trawler, or minesweeper, to take us south. So that's how we got away.

I had been made a medical officer, an acting medical officer—I was only a senior medical student—which came with a canteen of cognac as medical supplies. I arranged to sleep on board under a large coil of rope, and made myself cozy and slept there. Once in a while, but only once in a while, when everybody was asleep, and there was complete blackout, I used to take a little pull of cognac.

We crossed by way of French Morocco and arrived in Gibraltar. It was very reassuring to see two young male officers arrive in a little boat and just start distributing cigarettes.

We demonstrated what we could do with our ship's guns for the officers, and sat on board for a while, in fact, for two whole days. We saw the H.M.S. *Hood*, and the aircraft carrier *Ark Royal* leave harbor, and when they returned two days later, we found that they had neutralized the French fleet in Oran, which was being taken over by the Germans.

The Gibraltar commander offered our group posts as the crew of big fortress guns, because the British were very short handed, but our major decided we should fight a more active war, and go to England and fight. We transshipped from Gibraltar on a ship called *S.S.* Faubert; I believe that M. Faubert was the president of the shipping company. It was a 10,000 tonne ship, with us, some assorted Czechs and other loose groups on board. Our unit was the only organized one. We had morning and evening peals, kept fit, and manned the various machine guns and other assorted pieces for our ship's protection.

We left Gibraltar, I believe on July 1, and started on the long, slow sail from Gibraltar to England. We were shot at a few times by aircraft, and the one destroyer that was escorting our little convoy had its hands full with submarines, but we reached Liverpool somehow, and all in one piece. Life on that French ship wasn't bad. The cooks were fair, Czech cooks, and there was always some company, and not too much shooting. We arrived in Liverpool, and everything was very well organized. We got into the railway station, and there were long trays of bread and margarine and tea, everything neat and clean, and I just thought that I was in Paradise.

After we had enjoyed our little lunch, we got back on the train, but we didn't know where we were going, because everything was pretty much secret, and nobody was telling anybody anything. The location signs on all the stations were covered, so no one knew where they were going. We traveled fairly slowly overnight, with the good ladies of the W.B.S. distributing more bread and margarine and tea, until we arrived in Scotland. There, we were put on a truck, and driven a place called Douglas, a very pretty place in the Highlands, and we had nice, clean tents, where we could wash, bathe, and we were even given our first four shillings' pay, for a day, which was absolutely fabulous, because after the French pay of 50 centimes—half a penny—a day, four shillings was like a fortune.

I remember going to the Church of Scotland canteen in the camp, and eating several shillings' worth of canned pineapple and candy and milk. That was before the very strict rationing. You couldn't get those things over the next few days or months. It was almost like Paradise. And then we started training in Scotland.

For a while we didn't have any equipment, because everything was lost in Dunkirk; in fact, all the British equipment was gone. We trained the best we could. There were no more horses: everything was motorized, and our equipment, we had eleven rifles. That was supposed to be an artillery unit! We patrolled some dumps and power stations, and every night we'd change, with a different eleven guys going out on patrol. Eventually, we got a little more equipment but, unfortunately, we were transferred several kilometers away to a place was called Crawford, still in the Highlands.

Crawford was a very stupid camp. The camp was built—a tented camp—in a bowl, so whenever it rained, all the water came into the tents. After some time, we made some nice friends, and then we were moved to Dundee, and billeted in a school, in black, miserable Dundee. I spent some little time there, being again an acting medical officer; otherwise, I was running around with guns. Eventually, while in Dundee, we received our first for-real artillery weapons, four small howitzers. It was a great time.

There was one advantage to being under British command, and that was cleanliness. Everywhere we went, it was clean. This was much different from France, where—if you pardon the expression—we had lice. Lice are little animals that bite, particularly when it gets warm, and are rather unpleasant. We had been deloused a few times. Delousing meant having your uniform and clothes put into a steam laundry, and at the same time showering and washing to kill all the little animals. This was rather difficult in the winter, because the clothes were wet from steam, and the showers were cold.

We had very interesting exercises. Among other things, we had one civil defense exercise on being attacked by German aircraft in Dundee. It was a mock exercise, and we demonstrated all the wares we had in our sanitary units. Time went on, and there was more and more training. One sad event happened. A truck in our group turned over, and four of our cadets died within a couple of days.

Social life was very pleasant, if you could call it that. We had a few dances in our battery, and we also frequented a so-called glee house, which was a movie house with coffee, doughnuts and candy, used also as a little cafe. That's where we used to meet the local working female population.

After a short time, we were transferred to Montrose, and after a little training, attached to coastal guns. These were naval guns, which were converted to coastal defense. During that time, the summer of Britain ended. On one occasion, everybody was expecting an invasion, and our whole crew was sitting out in the rain in Scotland, waiting for the German paratroopers to turn up, but they didn't. Montrose was a very quiet place; we never had to fight there.

The Polish government was in exile and the British government, specifically the University of Edinburgh, set up a medical school for senior and final-year Polish students from the University of Warsaw and other universities. Against my inclinations, I applied. I really wanted to be a gunner, particularly with my feelings about the Nazis. However, I suppose I was sensible enough to do what I could do best. I applied for the final examinations at the University of Edinburgh, and I was accepted.

We had both Scottish and Polish professors and, basically, most of the main subjects were English, so we had to learn English posthaste. I went to Edinburgh, and led the student's life for a while. We were given permission to live in private British quarters for a few months, and after that, we were shepherded into a military hostel, and we all lived communally in one big house. It took me sixteen months to master English and pass my examinations. It was rather difficult; however, I had learned my English from the girls at the dance halls, like Palais de Danse and Plaza, and I managed to get by.

I liked forensic medicine, a regular University of Edinburgh course, best of all. The first graduate of that school was a man by the name of Konrad Pazanik. Konrad, who was a flyer, graduated in November of 1941, and was the first graduate of the Polish School of Medicine at the University of Edinburgh. After that, more of us graduated, and the next class, much larger, graduated in July 1942. The graduation ceremony was very impressive. My friend Jan Majeranowski was in that class.

My time in Edinburgh was very pleasant, compared to what everybody else was doing at that time. News from Poland was terrible, and spoiled everything, but we had to get our qualifications before going back to the army. Life in Edinburgh was very interesting. It was a beautiful city. Prince's Street, with modern buildings and stores on the left, and Edinburgh Castle on the right, was just beautiful. We used to go for lunches sometimes to the Castle. The Castle had a restaurant for the military, so I used to walk to the Castle once in a while, and have some toad-in-the-holes and sausages, and drink a little bit of milk, if it was available. Social life was much better at college than it was in France or in various other places in Scotland.

Stanley (right) and friend, Edinburgh, 15 July, 1942

During that time, I visited Uncle Henry in London. Unfortunately, he was seriously hurt in a bombing raid while going to his duties, and had a very bad leg fracture, which did not heal for about six months. I also visited Aunt Roma and Uncle Leonard Matters whom, while I was still in France and had nothing, managed to sneak me a pound or two now and then, which helped very greatly. In Edinburgh, the study was hard, but I learned a lot. In fact, when I was writing some of my qualifications in the United States and Canada, I still used materials which I learned in Poland and in Scotland. The teachers were good. Techniques were not so advanced, but their diagnosis and clinical instruction was excellent. In fact, when I was in the United States, somebody asked me, "Which school do you come from?" I said, "The best—Edinburgh, Scotland", and those people agreed.

I only failed one exam, out of about sixteen; I knew the material for that particular exam better than any other I did, so that's what I flunked. However, three months later, I was allowed to repeat, and I passed and graduated in July 1942, in the same group with Jan Majeranowski and a whole bunch of others. Quite a few of them are now in the United States, incidentally. And one—Dr. Maniets—became a professor of medicine in Ottawa.

After we graduated we were posted, but with no definite departure time. Waiting for transport, we took some training as interns in Western General Hospital in Edinburgh, which had one Polish wing. We'd go to Dundee or Edinburgh to meet friends and influence people, and wait for transport.

In Burntisland, a very interesting little city, there was a manor in which apparently Queen Mary Stuart slept on one occasion. Things hadn't changed much, because the washroom, the toilet, was in a kind of chute. There was no such thing as running water, but there was some water in basins.

Billeting us was quite profitable for the farmer, so we didn't tell anyone when we cracked a huge mirror in the main living room where we slept, the five of us. It was rather in the way for us to get to bed and out, so we pushed it behind the radiators, which were not on. Somebody turned on the heat and one night, we were in bed, and there was an almighty bang! We thought that somebody had dropped a bomb. But all that happened was that the mirror had cracked. I must confess, we felt rather embarrassed and didn't tell anybody, and just let it be.

Then, one day, we were told we are going to the Middle East.

CHAPTER FOUR

MIDDLE EAST

We were told we were going to the Middle East, and then we were told to wait, and wait. I kept going to the hospital every morning by train, to do a little more training, until one day, it was decided we were really going. We went to the Burntisland station and got on the train, and then the odyssey began.

We went all around Scotland, back and forth, and back and forth, probably to fool spies, who were looking for sea convoys. We went to the extreme east of Scotland, got switched around several lines, and off we went the other way, and we got off at Greenock, which is in the port of Glasgow.

We just walked up with our kits, and the seafaring people, who were managing the whole thing, said "O.K., this is your boat." Up we went, up the gangplank of quite a big ship, the *Empress of Scotland*. It was initially called the *Empress of Japan*, but in view of the Japanese attack on the British and Americans, the name was changed. It was a Canadian Pacific ship, about 35,000 tonnes. We boarded, and we sat on the ship for two days. Not at the dock, but moored out on the sea, on the ship. There were many convoys were being assembled there, and as we were moved out to our mooring, all the dockworkers cheered and shouted. Eventually, one morning, we woke up and couldn't see anything around, there was no more Glasgow, it was gone; we were really underway, we were at sea.

The weather was lousy. I figured we were going north, but of course, no information was given out in case of spies; which really did happen, it wasn't just a story, it was happening all the time. Then I thought we went toward Newfoundland, and then south. And that's the way we went, all the long way down south, to the South Atlantic, to Bahia [known today as Salvador; Bahia was the city's name during the eighteenth century], in Brazil. We had three troop ships, *The Empress of Scotland*, *Stirling Castle* and *Avalon Castle*, and two liners.

We saw a lot of interesting sights on our five week journey across the sea: whales, which in those days were not hunted, a lot of porpoises, some killer whales, and when we moved into the warm climate, lots of flying fishes. It's not true that flying fishes fly over the ships and settle; they generally fly below the level of the ship, and they go up to thirty or forty yards at a time. Very colourful. I was particularly fascinated watching the sea life, particularly the dolphins. They kept playing around the ship.

There were two doctors, with whom we traveled, with the very strange names of Wasciesz, pronounced "Washish", and Janikewicz, pronounced "Yanishevitch". These fellows were very good friends. They were about thirty-five years of age, and they always wore long shorts, being in tropical waters, which were not really properly done up, they were rather long. And they wore pith helmets, day and night, regardless. So we found Janikewicz and Wasciecz walking up and down on the deck in pitch darkness wearing their pith helmets, and discussing the affairs of the world.

We had a considerable escort with us—an armed merchant cruiser, two destroyers, and two frigates—because we had five troop ships, personnel only, with very little equipment. There were about three and a half thousand troops on *The Empress of Scotland*, and that involved sixteen physiotherapists, ladies who rehabilitated soldiers after injury. They all were very romantic in the darkness, or under the moon, but were they homely in the daylight! We met quite a few people, South Africans, Scots, British, and Polish. The food was good, and plentiful, and it was rather pleasant to be able to enjoy a sea journey, even under the circumstances. We played cards, mostly bridge. We walked up and down the deck and exercised, but we could only exercise so much, and just lazed around a lot. Just lazed around with submarine alerts interspersed about two or three times a week. Everybody had to put on their lifejackets and rush to the lifeboats. After we passed the inspection, we were back on our own.

It was quite fascinating to see tall palm trees sticking out of the surface of the water before we actually saw port or land; they were so tall, you could see the tops of them. We finally arrived, and were moored in the port city of Bahia [Salvador], which had as its old name El Salvador, midway on Brazil's coast, north of Rio. On the second day, we were allowed to disembark. We all had to be very well organized, and then we marched through the city. For a couple of hours we were released, and then we had to march back to the ship again. This happened three or four days in a row.

I stayed five days in Bahia, in the only Latin American country I ever visited. The Brazilians speak Portuguese, while most of the other South American nations speak Spanish. Brazil, at one time, even had an emperor, the Emperor of Brazil, who visited the United States, apparently a very friendly fellow. Bahia was not a pretty city. There was tropical vegetation and some very nice houses and buildings that were interesting, but it was a poor city. I believe all the wealth at that time was in Rio. The people were very friendly, and many of them could speak English, although I don't think that very many could speak Polish. They were friendly, and very direct. For example, if you met a group of men and women sitting in a cafe, drinking a cup of coffee, or possibly one of those horrible South American concoctions, one man might say, "Oh, I'm sorry, but I have to get my injection", which meant that he'd just announced to everybody that he's being treated for VD. So it was rather direct, and doctors for treatment of venereal disease were all over the place.

One morning, we woke up and were at sea again. There were more flying fishes, and more dolphins, and Janikewicz and Wasciecz still walking up and down with those pith helmets and the convoy traveled the South Atlantic fairly slowly. The only other things we saw were a few sharks, which we hadn't seen before. We played bridge and did some physical training, and talked and enjoyed the long evenings at sea until we started veering east, and we realized we were moving towards South Africa.

The whole trip to South Africa was relatively peaceful. There was far less bombing there than in Britain, but while we were moving towards Cape Town, we saw some of the war at sea. Our convoy picked up one castaway, who was floating on a wardrobe. All the sea was full of debris, pieces of furniture, and other bits and pieces from a ship that had been torpedoed by a German submarine off Cape Town.

We went on to Cape Town, but did not disembark there; we disembarked at Durban. This was a very, very pleasant city—beautiful—plenty of fruit, fresh fruit, for which we were all starved. We were located in a transit camp in Durban, and went to the city every day, and I met quite a few people. Amongst other friends, I met an engineer, whom I had known in Poland, outside the King Edward Hotel in Durban. We also had the Honorary Polish Consul in Poland, who was a very nice fellow, and his family spent a lot of time with us, and helped us around. For company, we had Canadian nurses from a South African hospital. It's rather amazing to think now, that in those days, in South Africa, you could buy a pineapple for tuppence, and a peach for a penny. We availed ourselves of that quite a bit. Durban was clean, very well built and an attractive city. I stayed in the camp, but we had some South African friends, and visited a lot, so we really just slept in the camp, and spent most of our weeks socializing.

We spent two weeks in the camp, and then back to the port by train, and onto a new ship, a Dutch ship of 39,000 tonnes, called the *New Amsterdam*. The ship was loaded with at least two shiploads of soldiers and went without a convoy, because it was a fast ship, faster than the submarines. So we took off from Durban, and it took us two weeks, fast steaming, to get Port Said in Egypt, by way of Suez. We saw a lot of sea life, and particularly sharks, which are more than plentiful there, and it was clear sailing to the Middle East.

We had some seven to eight thousand troops on board, and there was a whole South African brigade there, and these South Africans were extremely friendly. There was a little lounge to which I was privileged to attend because I was a commissioned officer since arriving in South Africa. We used to go to the small lounge, with all these hundreds of people, and line up, about six of us, and everybody bought six drinks, one for each. That was the only way to get a second drink, because the bar was open at 9:30, and by 10:30 that was it for the day. We bought several drinks each, slowly drinking them up. The food was good, the Dutch cooks and stewards were good, and the ship was certainly moving, regardless of stormy seas or anything else.

When we arrived in Port Said, we got off the ship with our kits, and we marched to the transit camp, and it was really very cold. It was December 31, 1942. We had the first British victory of the war at the big battle of El Alamein. In the transit camp, unfortunately, we had very little money, but we managed to get a drink on New Year's night. I had also developed one of the biggest backaches of all times. I don't know whether it was because I was carrying my kit, or because it was cold, or because it was so uncomfortable from sleeping on shelves in the transit camp.

We were soon put on a train, and went from Suez across Israel and Jordan, and then onto some trucks. On those trucks we traveled across the desert towards Iraq. Once the road ended, all the trucks fanned out and beat hell for leather across the desert. After a few days we reached Baghdad, the fifth city of fable, which looked, in the setting sun, like a city out of the Arabian Nights, with minarets, temples, and palaces—sunsets on the Tigris River—all very fascinating.

After just a very short stop and a look around, we were put on a train and traveled rather slowly north from Baghdad, closer to the Persian border, to a place called Khanaqin. Khanaqin was in the vicinity of the Iraqi oil fields, and was very close to the fairly tall Zagros Mountains, beyond which lay Persia, Iran. We saw a lot of Kurds there, a very independent tribe, who do not recognize either Iran or Iraq, and wanted their own independence. They had been fighting for it for about 100 years. The Kurds seemed like very fine people with beautiful, nicely bedecked horses, and long rifles. They were very friendly, so far as we were concerned, but I don't think they liked the Iraqis or the Persians very much.

In Khanaqin, we went through the normal, standard procedures of the Army. Somebody decided more doctors were needed than were actually needed and, as a result, some of us were left unemployed, just sitting in a base depot, spending our time shaving when there was water (we very often used tea for shaving), and eating rather poor fare. The commander of the depot, a Major Reichert, was a perfect example of a dumb, regular Polish officer. If there was somebody he could find to harass, he would.

We lived like that for a while until, through a friend, I got a job, and I was appointed as liaison officer to a British base in Habbaniyah, which was back about 80 miles west of Baghdad. I had some knowledge of English, and as the Polish units in that area were attached to the Habbaniyah air base, I got the job.

Four or five of us of us, officers who were working with the British Air Force, made the trip together. It was rather amazing, getting from Khanaqin back to Baghdad on the train; typical slumming, so to speak. Our RTO, Rail Transport Officer, did not arrange for reservations, so we managed to get into Arab fourth class. Very friendly, but very noisy and rather unwashed, with little animals like chickens and goats in the train with us. After a while we stopped, and we started talking to the Iraqi conductor. For a small gift, he opened up an official coach used by Iraqi dignitaries on train journeys. It was a palace; a complete dining room, lounge, bedroom, baths, and restaurant on the train. We had a very pleasant trip all that day, indeed. Unfortunately, drinking the Iraqi *arak*, which is a very potent drink, disagreed with most of us. The conductor also cooked us meals, and we had some sleep, and everybody had bad stomachs.

Arriving back in Baghdad again, we got off, and walked around the famous hotels and mosques, with their beautiful latticework and mosaics, which lined the bank of the river Tigris. Baghdad was really a very beautiful city, but it was dead unfortunately, and of course, poor. I bought a military belt, a so-called Sam Browne, which I had needed for some time, for a very low price, without haggling. There were practically no customs at that time in Iraq, so whatever was available, we could buy easily at a low price.

The British transportation arrived in the morning of the following day, and we went on to Habbaniyah, which was a big old British base, built in 1921. They had old silver in the officer's mess, beautiful baths, riding horses, anything that an expatriate could possibly require. The base consisted of a transport air base, with a little escort, antiaircraft batteries, barracks, messes, canteens, cinema and a hospital.

I was attached to the hospital, to care for the Polish patients. Most of the Poles at that time were freshly arrived from Russia, where they were allowed to leave from exile to join the forces to fight the Germans. So one enemy let them go in order to fight the other enemy. There was a pretty good Polish wing in the hospital, and the Polish component in the place was an anti-aircraft battery. I was also attached as a general duty medical officer, so I was looking after all kinds of patients, and was also running nightly calls, as necessary, when I was in charge of the whole hospital.

There were a whole bunch of Commonwealth medical doctors there and, fortunately, Commonwealth nurses as well. The hospital commander and the Group Captain had the name of A. C. K. H. Foreman. I also met some other interesting people, like Ted Spence, who immediately before the war was the tennis champion of South Africa. Also a dermatologist by the name of Davis, and Captain Buckley, who was a champion ground hockey player, and there were two surgeons, Samuel—whose name I don't recollect—and then more junior was Wing Commander Arden. And my bearer, whose name was Haji, was a very nice, unassuming man, quiet, and very, very efficient. Anything that I needed done he did very quietly, usually ordering his own juniors to do the work, but he was managing everything, and making sure I was happy.

We'd go to the movies once in a while, and there were also horse races there, on a very small scale; mostly Arab riders with their horses. Once in a while, an officer who particularly wanting to be a sportsman, bought the winning horse. Two fellows, one was a dental officer, and another fellow, they had one horse between the two of them, and there was always a big argument between them about whose end came first, the front end or the back end. Habbaniyah was a very pleasant base. I enjoyed it, I enjoyed the people, and I made some good, fast friendships.

I worked as medical liaison office for some seven months to the British base in Habbaniyah. It was all very pleasant; however, nothing is perfect, and I got sick, and I was in the hospital for five weeks, and eventually evacuated to Egypt.

CHAPTER FIVE

EGYPT

I had a bronchoscopy, received treatment for dysentery and malaria, and I couldn't have gotten sick at a better time. I had requested a transfer to other British units, and this was not very popular with my chief. I knew my job in Habbaniyah was coming to an end, the unit was going to move on and I would no longer be a medical officer there, so I wrote an application to be attached to the Air Force, not the Polish Army. Unfortunately, I sent it through my commanding officer and Group Captain Foreman, as I was instructed, and the great big blow-up in the Polish units then was about the guy trying to go to work for the British. So I was sent to sit in a hospital in Egypt and have various procedures done. I saw my first case of a death to sulfa drugs there. A very nice officer who got tonsillitis; he was given Sulfanilamide, and died as the result of side effects.

I was in Egypt in the hospital for six weeks or longer before I was allowed to go out for several hours a day. I'd to go to a place called the Heliopolis Swimming Club, to sit in the hot Egyptian summer, in the club, and drink shandy, which is half-and-half beer and lemonade. The best Egyptian beer was called Stella and was very strong. I also used to go to a very superior club, for Egyptian aristocracy and British officers, and watch cricket games, whenever I wasn't asleep in a deck chair. Just clapping your hands would bring a silent drink. Have a drink, watch some of the others, and then back to the hospital to be sick again. It was very nice, I even got introduced to King Farouk. He was a very fat man who used to be the king of Egypt.

However, all good things must come to an end and I got better and went to a transit camp, with probable evacuation to Britain. However, before the evacuation started, my old Polish colonel sent for me to come to Palestine. So I went back to a hospital in Palestine—now Israel—about a hundred kilometers from Tel Aviv. The place, I think, was called Gezira.

So I sat there and visited Tel Aviv, a rather bustling city, once a week on a bus. I met a lot of people there, mostly British, New Zealanders and Australians, and some South Africans. I visited Jerusalem, a very interesting city, and saw the famous Wailing Wall. I was an ordinary medical officer in Palestine, going once a week to Tel Aviv, then back again for a while.

Tel Aviv was a very pleasant city with good restaurants and good facilities, but hotel accommodations were almost nonexistent. We used to double—and triple-up in each room. Once I was lucky, and got a room to myself in the officers' club, but that was only once. I went to an officers' shop in Gedera, and purchased a folding chair and a sleeping bag; also a pair of light leather boots, to go about in instead of the desert boots I had been wearing in the desert.

I had a fairly pleasant time; I saw various people, the local Jewish community and, of course, all the other Allied troops. I particularly remember coming into a Greek restaurant in Jerusalem, it was a very pleasant one, with a bar, and having a drink with a friend of mine, an old, old ack-ack man whom I knew before the war (I believe he lived in South Africa afterwards). We went to the bar and bought ourselves a little drink and were talking, and then a rather gray-haired Australian, a captain or major, started talking with us. Australians and Poles were together in the Tobruk siege in 1940-41, and they spent together, I think, something like 91 days. So he started talking to us and buying drinks and in the meantime another officer came and said "Look, your girl's waiting for you." And he said, "To hell with her! I have two Poles to drink with!" So, we sat and drank and talked and we chewed the fat and eventually he left. Whether he ever found that girl again or not, I don't know.

I managed to get some billet and sleep overnight in Jerusalem, and then I went back to camp, and worked there. It was very cold, strangely enough, because it was coming towards the late fall, and Palestine was not particularly warm at this time, particularly outside, away from the sea. I had a place there, a very, very small kind of hole, some distance from showers and other facilities. I had my own camp bed, and chair. Of course, we had a mess at the hospital, where they served three, sometimes four meals a day.

I was looking at wards, and inspecting the patients; once in a while, I had to inspect the kitchens. It was not a terribly attractive part-time job until I got attached, as one of my duties, to visit the ATS wards, Auxiliary Territorial Service, which were mostly female drivers and female clerks. I was the first male medical officer they'd ever had, so they put on an awful lot of cosmetics, extra nighties, and so on. At twenty-six years old, that was my "bright fifteen minutes" of the day. Very few of them were really ill.

The mess was quite pleasant; there were a good bunch of medical officers, particularly Major Tippelt; strangely enough, he used to tipple, but his name was Tippelt. I worked there for some time and got to know a whole bunch of other people. I had a friend who was a great archaeologist and geographer, and he organized all kinds of tours. He got a group to go to Jerusalem, and visit the Holy Sepulchre and the Church of the Nativity, and several other places. In the Church of the Holy Sepulcher, which had been in power since the Crusades, we saw a very remarkable sight. Three very, very fat Arabs in fezzes sitting in an ancient big, fat settee, sitting there, and keeping guard against the infidels. They didn't bother anybody, so we went in, and it was a most impressive visit.

The church was divided into all major faiths. There was, of course, the Roman Catholic section, the largest of all was the Greek Catholic Church section, there was a Coptic section, and several others. We had a guide, who showed us all the things, and fortunately, the place was not yet commercialized; it was extremely impressive. Some of the parts of the original Sepulchre had been incorporated into the present edifice. Legend says that on this particular stone sat the guardian angel guarding the mother of Jesus. Another legend says that in Calvary, the drops of blood of Jesus were dripping through the cave on the skull of Adam, which, I think, is a very beautiful legend. This was a very, very impressive and uplifting experience, even though some of the minor faiths tried to cash in a little to help themselves keep up their sections.

We went to the Church of the Nativity, which was actually at Christmas, and there were masses and masses of people; it was just one sea of faces. The church was packed. There was the usual Christmas Mass, and choirs, wondrous smells, and organ music. Nobody could kneel because the place was so packed; there was no way anybody could kneel because they couldn't get up again. After that, we went and saw several other places. One of them was Bethlehem. We walked around Calvary, and then finally, after a second visit to the Church of the Nativity, we walked through the Via Dolorosa, the crucifixion route, and then we went back to camp. It was an experience you usually don't get even once in a lifetime.

After that, we just worked, we went nowhere, as far as Palestine was concerned; we just worked in the camp, and back in Tel Aviv once in a while, until our hospital was transferred, and we were moved to Ismailia, which was in Egypt. This only involved crossing the Suez Canal, which wasn't very far.

Ismailia was a real desert location. There were no major cities anywhere nearby. There was a town, which had a French club, and a few restaurants, but not much else. The greatest attraction was watching the traffic on the Suez Canal. It almost appeared, looking from the camp, that the ships were moving across dry land—a funny optical illusion. There was nothing particularly attractive there otherwise. The French club was quite nice, and once in a while, we made up a group of four to six doctors and nurses, and went out to dinner.

Before I moved out, I managed to arrange, with my Jerusalem trip friend, for a trip around Egypt. We went by train south to Luxor, a fairly good all night train trip, and saw the pyramids and the Sphinx from a distance. On arriving at the Luxor Hotel, we immediately arranged for guides and their very ancient cars to take us around. We started by seeing the Temple of Luxor, which I believe was Ramses II, and the Egyptian architecture was absolutely stupendous. Against those four thousand years-old columns, people looked just like flies on the wall. However it was built, I don't know, but they did it.

The Temple of Luxor was distinguished by having a double row of sphinxes with ram's heads. There was an awful lot of original carvings on the Temple of Luxor, as indeed in every other major Egyptian temple that we visited. There was a lot of Egyptian history there. For example, there is a huge temple which wasn't completely finished by a Pharaoh named Taharka, who was a Nubian, and was attempting to revive the Egyptian conquests. He died in 663, BC, and he didn't do much, except make sure the conquest of Egypt by Nubia was maintained.

The first evening, we spent in an Egyptian dhow on the Nile, just sitting on the benches, and admiring the Egyptian night. The next day, we saw Rameseum, the Temple of Queen Hatshepsut, and visited the tombs and statues. Rameseum was a very massive structure, not quite as massive as Luxor, but still very big indeed, with lots of carvings, some of them depicting life in Egypt, some depicting battles and the exploits of Pharaohs and other commanders. Very secretly, our Arab guide, who stayed with us throughout the week, brought the men together, and he took us to one of the carvings, the Battle of Kadesh, Ramses II, and showed us where they cut off all the genitals of the enemy. It was rather funny when one of the nurses came and said, "Oh, this is the sausage factory!"

There were masses of other carvings, a lot of them of sexual connotation. The main god of Egypt was Amen Ra, and he was also the sex symbol, and some of the carvings depict offerings made to him. We saw, nearby, apparently the oldest carvings in New Egypt, the temple of goddess Sekhmet, who was depicted as a woman with a lioness' head. She stood alone in a small, very heavily bordered chamber, in semidarkness, and I could not help feeling, even though she looked so grim, that she was very alone, and I felt sorry for her. Then, we saw Memnon's Colossi, which were two colossal statues in a sitting position, possibly depicting Ramses II, but nobody was really quite certain about it. The interesting thing about Memnon's Colossi, was that when there was a slight wind, they sounded almost like music. They emitted the sound of, like a wailing violin. They just stood up out the desert, there were no any other real surroundings, and the statues were very weathered.

We saw the temple of Queen Hatshepsut. She was quite an interesting lady, who ruled during the XVIII dynasty, an early women's libber. She assumed the title of Pharaoh, and even had a little beard made, which she wore while on official duties, so that she had the appearance of a male Pharaoh. She was, apparently, quite a tart cookie, and it seems that her son, who succeeded her, hated her, and had her likeness knocked out of all the temples, and statues, after her death, so all that's left is just the one depiction of Queen Hatshepsut in the tenth temple, which somehow escaped the hammer and chisel. The temple itself was not as imposing as those of the Ramses, but it was, I would say, more artistic; more slender, and perhaps a little more modern in outline.

Then we started for the Valley of the Kings. That was, essentially, like visiting old tombs. The interesting thing was that only one tomb escaped the grave robbers, and that was the tomb of Tutankhamen. We saw several others, the tomb of Ramses, Ramses II, and the tombs of common officers. They were quite strenuous visits, because there was no air conditioning, and those deep tombs in the Egyptian desert, going down to maybe ten meters, were pretty stuffy. In the tombs were paintings, and what was absolutely amazing was the quality of them. The mystery of the dyes that the Egyptians used still was unknown when I was there, but they looked like modern paintings, as far as the quality is concerned; they certainly were not oil, they were some sort of dry paint.

We learned a lot about Egyptian life from the tombs, because they showed their agriculture, they showed their military, they showed their religion, they showed even collecting taxes and the actions of judges; it was all depicted in the tombs. And there were some artifacts in the tombs of lesser nobles that were not entirely robbed. They kept small statuettes, usually wooden, of various workers, slaves, soldiers, model boats, model carriages, paintings of cattle, all rather interesting, that they were supposed to have been prepared for the noble or pharaoh for later life, so that he would have his court with him, and not be by himself. And that was why, I thought, the Egyptians loved their daily life more than the Greeks ever did, because the Egyptians believed in the immortal soul, and the Greeks didn't. The Valley of the Kings was one of the greatest experiences, because I just could not believe it all was four thousand years old.

After we left the Valley of the Kings, we had one more day in the area, to see a couple more temples. One of them was Edfu temple, which was partly submerged after the building of the first Aswan dam. Then a few minor temples, and we returned to Luxor, and late at night we got on the train and went to Aswan, the site of the great dam, built by the British in the earlier days. Later, in the 1950's, the Russians built a new dam, which completely dwarfed the great Aswan dam. It was still pretty impressive when I was there. There were big sluices to control the flooding. When the Russians built the great dam, it was supposed to be a great boon to Egyptian agriculture, and irrigation. Initially, it was, but what was happening was that the dam was so big and powerful it carried away too much silt, the lifeblood of the fertile Egyptian delta valley, and they were beginning to worry seriously about what would happen when the silt ran out. It could possibly turn, after thousands of years of agricultural fertility, into another desert!

There were many interesting things in Egypt. A temple was supposed to be submerged with the building of the second new dam, but through international efforts, it was raised, and saved for posterity, which I think was a pretty good thing, because ancient Egypt can never be replaced. There were ancient water wheels, with a poor donkey going in circles, pumping water. There was a relatively small canal, oh, maybe ten, fifteen meters across, which went all the way from Ismailia to Luxor, and was supposedly dug by the Israelites during the Egyptian captivity just before the days of Moses.

So we spent a little while in Aswan, this was in February of 1944, but many beautiful things don't last very long. We went back to Egypt, back to Ismailia, and we sat having our good times in the hospital, bored but peaceful. The social life wasn't too bad; good dinners at the French club, and not expensive, either. One day the news came, four officers were to be removed to Italy. I was the only one from our hospital to be posted so, in early May 1944, I put my kit on and was driven to Cairo, on my way to Italy.

CHAPTER SIX

ITALY

I met three other officers, from different units, who were also going to Italy. We put up in the officers' hotel, and sat in Cairo waiting for transportation. In the meantime, we went to see the Egyptian cabaret, very oriental, and ate crevettes in groppis, which were excellent. At about three or four o'clock in the morning we were awakened, and told to get transportation to the airport. There were three of us, one of whom was the cousin of the automobile champion whom I'd met before in Rumania, and this one was at one time the heavyweight boxing champion of Poland.

We were driven to Heliopolis airport, and got on a DC-3, which was called a Dakota in those days, all aluminum plated, for paratroops, and we got on, each with a box of groppis chocolate (those chocolates were really good), and off we took from Cairo. The first stop was in Tobruk, where we had about twenty minutes for lunch and to refuel. The second stop was in Malta, where we could still see the ravages of the recent bombing. The third stop was Italy. We flew in at about 14,000 feet, with a bunch of flyers on the plane, and one of them must have been a fighter pilot, because he said he was going to land that thing. When he took the controls, I thought it was the end, because he took us straight down, but it was just his ebullient spirits, being a fighter pilot and flying a slow, old plane. So we landed in a place called Bari, Italy.

Bari was supposed to be an Italian Babylon, but not that I noticed it. Babylon lasted about two days; it was a nice place, but it was just too full of soldiers, and their general was not terribly nice. Again, I went to camp, and I sat in another base depot for another week. In the meantime a heavy battle had started, and fortunately, I did get to a good unit. I was supposed to do liaison work again with the Polish and British units, but there was some snafu, and I ended up as a medical officer in an infantry battalion, the 13th Infantry Battalion, Fourth Polish Infantry Division, with whom I spent all the rest of my active duty. That division was organized mostly from Poles who managed to escape from Russia; they were good guys. So, I arrived, and that was where the war started as far as I was concerned, in Italy, because in the other places, other than Poland and France, and a few Battle of Britain episodes, I hadn't had any real war, so to speak, not fighting war.

Our infantry battalions were crack units, generally fighting most of the time. I always tried to be with the men, because I had an idea, from previous military experience, that if you were close to your troops you were one hell of a lot safer than back at headquarters, where you often got heavy bombardment. I used to try to set up my aid station anywhere from 100 to 200 yards from the line. That gave the men some sense of security; they knew that they could be killed, but they also knew that if they didn't get killed, but only wounded, they could get some help fast.

I made a very good bunch of friends there, both officers and noncommissioned officers; of course, on that line, there were no nurses. We had fairly heavy losses. Very soon I started losing friends. I never got hit myself; I got a cracked leg, but I wasn't shot. I was lucky, because we had been shelled and shot at; some didn't do so well. I lost several noncommissioned officers, and, of course, quite a few officers and other friends. Our battalion, which was supposed to be about 600 men, had less than 250 by the time we ended the May part of the campaign. Fortunately, many of them came back, and most of them survived.

To give an idea of what was happening to us, at the Battle of Cassino, our division— and our divisions were small, they weren't very big divisions—lost 1500 killed. I lost one young doctor friend there, and a few others. Actually, I got into this particular unit because the previous medical officer, strangely enough, was a regular army officer, not a reservist, and cracked up, so they sent him back, and I came in. Of course, I was under some pressure to maintain the standard, but I had been told that I was crazy, so it must have been all right.

That phase of the campaign was an odd and unpleasant one. The terrain was up and down; it was a lot of hills. Small engagements and you take one hill, and here they are over the other hill, and you've got to take the other hill, and so it goes. Each time you lose one or two men, who are killed or wounded. The Battle of Ancona was one major one, and cost 41 killed, half of the losses our battalion suffered in the second Battle of Cassino. Lost one or two friends, notably Lieutenant Sinkiewicz (pronounced Shinkyevitch), who was a good friend of mine; in fact, we played cards the night before he was killed.

We kept plodding on after Ancona for a while, until we reached Pesaro, north of Ancona, and then the losses were so high, that the battalion could not perform effectively any longer, and we were pulled out to further towns on the Adriatic coast, outside the artillery range, and had some rest. It was something like 13 days to bring in the reinforcements, and train and replace some of the men. We stayed in various Italian places, notably Sant'Elpidio a Mare, which was a village, or very small town, with a very friendly Italian population, nice weather, and reasonable quarters. Our messing officer arranged for some extra food. We socialized with the Italians, and generally found it a very, very welcome respite.

Sant'Elpidio was a small place, but the people were extremely friendly. They sat in little taverns and discussed politics. I picked up a little bit of Italian, and it was very obvious that, after Mussolini's debacle, the people who were keeping the country going were women, who kept their families and kept their miserable economics somehow going, and were always well-dressed and pleasant and smart. The men were not nearly as nice or as civilized. One could see the disasters befalling a defeated nation like Italy. Beautiful buildings and good public works, a lot of that destroyed. Population demoralized. Little food, and general disintegration. The fact was that, on a lot smaller scale, the same sort of thing was happening to us.

The time came, and it was back to work. We started out again, and this time, we moved what was left of our battalion to Highway 9, which was east to west, and moved far inland, no longer on the Adriatic coast. And again, the same slogging march started. We had our battalions organized so that our brigade, the 13th Battalion, was used as a battering ram. When we broke through, the 14th Battalion exploited, with the 15th Battalion in reserve. The immediate losses were hardest on us, because we had to attack direct.

When we got to the plain of northern Italy, about Forli, we came out of the mountains, and saw a rather wide plain, and we could see, almost like on a map, the gun positions, the fire lines, and firing itself. We started from a place called Forlimpopoli, which we took, and then we went on to Forli, and kept on going to Frieze, until we stopped for a while, and went into the hills.

That was quite an interesting operation. We started at eight o'clock at night, and after the first 15 minutes, I thought I was just never going to make it, because we were absolutely mired in mud; mud in Italy could be terrible. Somehow, I got out, and got onto firmer ground, and on we went. It was pitch black, it was raining, and we didn't know where we were going, which sounds funny, but it wasn't. After a while, we started walking by following our mules; we followed the mule's tail, and let the mule pick its own way. That was generally quite successful; I don't think anybody fell down or fell off. Our whole battalion went through the back of the German line, and we were more or less on our own. At one point, we could hear a great crashing noise. One of the mules carrying equipment, particularly stretchers, rolled over and went down the hill. Of course, there was no way to retrieve the mule, because it was too dark, and we just had to keep going. So we kept going. There was a little bit of fighting, and some friends got shot.

My commanding officer and another officer and two NCO's were wounded when, between the four of them, they attacked a German-held farm, and the Germans tossed a few hand grenades at them. Major Kowalczynski had a beautiful hole in his backside, and the others had assorted injuries. Being prepared for this type of action, we mobilized the stretcher bearers, who in their spare time were truck drivers, and we rushed to find them, and bring them back. That was a picture of misery; four men lying bleeding on the two big beds in that farmhouse. We dressed them up, and got them out, pushing them as fast as we could.

Finally, towards morning, we got out of the darkness and arrived in a place, which I could not name at all, but it was a farm on a hill. We set up our headquarters and medical station, all in the farmhouse. I had a number of wounded; six or seven seriously. One of them was beginning to develop gas gangrene, and two were shot in the brain. At that time, we could not evacuate casualties, because we were at the back of the German lines; we were more or less surrounded, so we helped them the best we could. Unfortunately, one of those, who had a serious brain wound, died. The man with gas gangrene survived, and was eventually evacuated home, with a minor paralysis of his right hand.

We sat there for a couple of days, and on the second day, we suddenly realized Peter wasn't there; he was lost. Peter was my orderly (a medical officer was entitled to an orderly in view of the type of work; one soldier, not usually too bright, was used to take care of the medical officer, make sure he got some food, a place to sleep, and so on). Peter was a very poor boy from eastern Poland but as good and honest as you could find, a very good fellow. I made some inquiries, from other soldiers, and discovered that Peter had apparently decided that the doctor didn't have his cigarettes, or his greatcoat, and he might be cold. He rolled up my greatcoat and took his cigarettes and started walking to find me, so that I wouldn't get cold, and walked straight into the German line. He was taken prisoner. That was the first time the Germans in that small area knew we had a whole battalion there, and they started withdrawing.

Fortunately Peter survived, even though the Germans stripped him of any little treasures he may have had, and I found him in England after the war, after he was liberated. It was really nice to see him.

I had my first and only major command during this action. With everybody engaged, there was a group of Germans in the woods who were still shooting, so we organized all the cooks, stretcher bearers, supply people and formed them into a unit, and we went after them and got them. Those we captured we sent off back.

After that, the orders came that the unit was to move to another location. By that time we had organized the casualties and sent them off with one or two trusty NCO's, the area never being really secured. We started marching, and I was in charge, because there was only three officers—myself and a British artillery observer and the regimental padre. Being infantry of sorts, I had to be put in charge of the whole thing. We didn't have the foggiest idea where we were going, but we walked and we arrived in a village with houses. We set up a little patrol, about four of us, and we busted in a door to find out who was occupying the village. There was very surprised group of Italians saying there was nothing going on there. That was absolutely wonderful news; we nearly kissed them.

We went on into the village and set up a proper aid station, in an old cafe. We cleaned it up; my boys were terrific at cleaning anything from a stable to a barn very nicely, and into a real medical unit. After all this we went to sleep, but wouldn't you know, my major from the brigade, Major Swieda (pronounced Shweeduh) arrived and started upbraiding me about the use of the stretcher-bearers. That was the one time I really blew my top, and I told him to go away and let me sleep, because I knew perfectly well what I was doing, and he didn't. He left, and I never heard from him again for some time.

Shortly after that, though, I got a medal, which was rather funny. I didn't get anything except a thank you for pulling the commanding officer out of the mess, but on another occasion when we were being shelled quite heavily, and I was sitting in a hole writing a letter to my girlfriend, a few wounded arrived, and I got mad so I got out and started shouting and screaming and upbraiding everybody to get those people evacuated. "Get them on! Get them out!" We got them out, and I got a medal, not for working but for screaming. Some of the guys who were wounded in that group had to be evacuated, and they went to hospital and, wondrously, they all came back. I think they survived the whole war.

We kept plodding along the hills above the plain, for two or three more weeks. By then Florence was occupied, but Bologna wasn't, and we sat on the Senio River where we spent two or three months, on a fixed line, behind the earth walls by the river. Every time we were in a jeep the Germans could see the top of the it, and they fired at us like blazes, but very seldom would anything happen because a jeep is not big enough to shoot, and the artillery and light weapon fire would go over the wall so, really, it was fairly safe.

Then I was given leave and the new Medical Officer, who replaced me, was a greenhorn, so I'm afraid I was a little naughty because I decided to show him the line. We got in the jeep and drove along the wall, and as long as we were driving the Germans were shooting. Of course, he was pretty scared, not being very experienced in this particular activity. However, I explained to him that as long as we were behind the wall we were not going to get hit, and he perked up considerably.

I went on leave with the same friend with whom I traveled in Egypt to Luxor, the great archaeologist. I had a vehicle, being a regimental man, and he was in the hospital, so he didn't have any transportation. We drove down to southern Italy, picked him up, and we drove to Naples and Rome. That was the highlight of my time in Italy; it was very beautiful. It was quite a long drive, because my friend's hospital was a base hospital right down in central Italy, and we had to pick him up in Riolene, so we drove quite a bit, and then we started up towards Rome on the east coast. It was rather interesting that while on the west coast, where the British and Canadians were fighting, the damage was far less than on the east coast, where the Americans were fighting, because they used heavy firepower to a much larger extent than we did. Whether that made any difference to casualties, I don't know, but everything was practically wrecked along the coast in that area.

We arrived in Naples, which was in rather poor shape. It had not been destroyed, but the economic situation of the people was very bad. The Allied troops and UNRRA (United Nations Relief and Rehabilitation Administration) were helping the best they could, but there was a lot of poverty and hunger. Naples itself was a beautiful city, but Capri was out of bounds, because there was a base there. I went to see La Scala, but the performance was not taking place; they hadn't reopened yet. Then we went, after driving around Naples, to Montevomero, which was just at the base of Vesuvius, in a little village on the coast, and there were some most beautiful little artifacts there, cameos made of lava, with beautiful workmanship but less color than the red and white ones in jewelry stores. We went to see Castel Sant'Elmo, which was a medieval fortress, dating to about the fourteenth century where, like in the old British castles, the horses and riders rode into the top of the castle. They had a military radio station right on top. That was a very interesting experience.

After Montevomero, we came down and looked a little more around Naples, and we continued north until we arrived in Rome. We saw St. Peter's Basilica, which was quite magnificent, and one interesting point there was St. Peter's statue, with one foot of the statue, which was made of bronze, worn smooth by the kisses of the faithful who kissed the statue going in. We went to the Vatican, which was very memorable because this friend of mine was a correspondent with a monsignor who was the librarian of the Vatican Library, and he showed us a lot of interesting documents including papal bulls of the thirteenth century. We saw the Sistine Chapel, and also visited the Vatican Museum, which was magnificent. I particularly remember a statue of St. Bernard defeating the devil, which was quite different from St. George. St. George was brash and very militant. St. Bernard stood there, in a semi-sitting position, holding the devil's leg with one hand. He looked very, very sad and pensive; he hadn't won the battle, he was just holding it off.

I didn't mention the ancient Roman antiquities, that is, the Roman Forum, various temples, and the Capitol, and other places, such as Caracalla's Baths, the great Roman bath of Emperor Caracalla. The Forum, somehow, was a little less impressive to me than Egyptian antiquities. They were not quite so imposing, they were more filigree, but still quite impressive. The Forum itself is not a very big place. It just about fits in a big city block. Caracalla's Baths were amazing. I don't know how they operated when they were used, but an awful lot of people could bathe there at the same time. The Romans really knew how to enjoy themselves. They had plumbing; the aqueducts were beautiful works of engineering. They used lead pipes, and the story is that as the educated classes and patricians and military had lead pipes, they were also subject to lead poisoning, and that contributed to early the mortality of these educated people.

After the Vatican we spent three days in Rome just enjoying ourselves, more or less. There were some places with good food and a few clubs, and little cafes, and espressos in the Piazza d'Espagna, which was a big place in Rome, a big place, and a square with little steps. Not too far from there was the Fontana di Trevi, in which people threw coins. We also saw some of the antiquities, which were not in the Vatican, like Moses' statue. Altogether, a very memorable experience. I wouldn't have missed it. We also saw Michelangelo's *Last Judgement*, which cannot be described but has to be seen. It was absolutely magnificent.

We finally we left Rome, left the nice Hotel Bologna, and we drove out and went to Livorno, or Leghorn, and to Pisa. First we stopped at the Leaning Tower of Pisa, which was really leaning, and we walked up the campanile, and it was quite a climb there; you've got to be careful not to topple over when you walk down. They say this thing is going to, sooner or later, topple over because, apparently, it is leaning a little bit more, a millimeter or so, every year, and then there will be no more Tower of Pisa. I hope that someone will save it, because it's a very interesting situation. The Leaning Tower of Pisa is not the cathedral itself, but is the campanile, the bell part of it. The cathedral itself is straight.

Well, all good things come to an end, so we started back. We dropped my friend off back in southern Italy and beat it posthaste to rejoin the unit because a big offensive was mounting, and we all felt that it would the last offensive and the war would soon be over. At one place in the hills, during the shelling, a dog attached itself to us. It was a beautiful German shepherd, with a reddish hue, which must have previously belonged to a German officer or NCO. He kind of befriended us, and we gave him some food and he stayed with us about two days, and then, at one time, there was a sudden burst of shelling, and as the shells came down, the dog took off very fast and we never saw him again. I was sorry; I was hoping that I might be able to keep him.

Finally, with many trials and tribulations, I returned to my unit, and took over again. Stenon Badowski, our photographer, was out looking for a sniper, who was picking off our fellows, and he found the sniper, but the sniper shot him and, while it appeared not to be a very serious wound, the next day he died. After that we got news that there was going to be a big push and that this may end the war in Italy. There were a lot of meetings and instructions, and getting equipment and training, all on the Senio River. Then we got our marching orders, that artillery preparation will be such-and-such time, air preparation will be such-and-such time, and the push would start at such-and-such time.

The night before we moved up to our jumping-off base, I was very careful about one particular thing. I had aircraft, air raid, shelters dug for everybody because one of the worst episodes of that campaign was when we got bombed by our own planes by mistake. So we dug those holes, and that was around three o'clock in the morning. At that time we were ahead of the forward units, so once we dug our holes and sat there, we sat there until the troops came up, which they did on time.

Then started the air bombardment. We sat in the holes (I didn't get hit), there was a short lull and then the artillery started, and only fired for about fifteen minutes of concentrated fire. And then all the boys got up, and we just went. We could see the Germans over the hill. We started moving up near them and there was some shooting. The Germans fought very well; they were very efficient. That's where I lost a young friend who was probably three or four years younger than I. He attacked a little unit, and the Germans raised their hands and surrendered, and when he came up one of them shot him in the forehead. And, sad to say, that particular company took 34 Germans, but only 3 of them survived after the episode.

That battle on Senio River, I think it was on April 13, was quite bloody. The Germans were somewhat fortified and they were very good fighters, and used their firepower to the best even though, at that stage, they often dragged their artillery by cow transport. Eventually that all stopped. We looked at our losses. There was one unit which was the Polish commanders, and commanders unfortunately had the idea that they were invulnerable, so when they started bringing their carriers and holding their heads high there was a terrible slaughter, including their padre who was picking up the wounded when he was shot. Eventually everything settled as well as it could be settled, and the wounded were evacuated.

We had been fighting solidly for about 14 hours, and I have to admit I got a little bit stoned because, at that stage, I had lots of supplies, plenty of booze, big clay jars with drinks for the wounded (the ones who were not shot in the stomach, no abdominal wounds). Whenever a boy was brought in who was in reasonable shape he got a shot of scotch or rum or gin, and I got a shot too of course. I had lots of cigarettes too, and each of them got at least a pack of cigarettes, and they were very happy and thought the war was going quite well.

Eventually we got to our destination, so to speak, and we settled for the bivouac, a partly fortified bivouac, because we didn't know whether there was much more fighting or not. Again our battalion and brigade took the biggest pounding of all the units, so we settled, and there was a battle, and we exploited, and we finished by April 23 or 24.

Other units began exploiting and going to Bologna. We didn't receive any orders to move on to Bologna, but other units were entering Bologna so we decided to go too. The C.O. and myself and two others drove into Bologna just about half an hour after it was liberated, and that was quite a time. The Italians were cheering and whooping and hollering, and kissing us, throwing flowers, and everything else. They had very little, but they were joyful. We met a few friends even, and then we kept driving through the city, and walking, and at one point, there was a great cry: "Il Garibaldidi!" Those were the last veterans of Garibaldi's campaigns. They must have been at least ninety years old each, three of them, and they came up feebly, with their Italian flag, so we saluted them, and there was another big cheer.

I met two or three very nice Italian analysts with whom I kept in touch for maybe a couple of years. After a while we found something to eat, and we went back to camp, which was maybe thirty kilometers away, and I went into Bologna the next day when everything settled. I made some more friends and had a meal, my last private meal in an Italian restaurant for the rest of the war because as soon as the military government, the UNRRA, came in they put on strict food rationing, and there were no private restaurants open. It was in a basement restaurant, and I remember what I had, I had pigs' ear, and believe it or not it was delicious.

I walked around Bologna and went to the university. I was very sorry to see that the medical school, with its famous anatomical museum, was busted but, fortunately, later on it was restored. The Germans had bombed the rail yards in Bologna, and that's where the damage came from.

We were looking at villages, and there was usually something beautiful in every village there. I remember a cathedral in Altamura, which is a tiny village in southern Italy, almost in Calabria. That tiny village there, not very clean, had the most beautiful cathedral. Quite tall, Romanesque style, with beautiful gargoyles. And there were very many places like that in Italy where, out of nowhere, something imposing and beautiful happened. Then we spent a little more time in Bologna; of course, we saw the Bologna cathedral, which was somewhat damaged at the time, and we sat there maintaining some training, because the situation was still pretty tricky, and the Russians and the Americans and the British met together. No one knew quite what was going to happen, but there were no major blow-ups, so everyone got friendly for a while.

We sat there spending our time, shooting at old beer cans with our pistols, training a bit, setting up exercises, because it was rather important to keep the troops occupied when in garrison in a foreign country; otherwise, the main problem became VD. It was June already, and we had a very sad event. Our padre, Father Bikowski, was killed after the war. We were still sitting pretty close to Bologna at that time, and what happened was he was blown up on a mine. Now, this padre was an interesting individual. Small, wiry, full of bounce, he had initially started in a seminary in Rome but during the war, once the British troops came into southern Italy, he crossed lines and joined the forces. He always wore a pair of long cavalry boots and generally behaved much more like a cavalry officer than like a padre. His favorite pastime was to get on a carrier and pick up the wounded in action. Also, once in a while, he went and fired mortars.

That day he, who was a very inquisitive individual, arranged to see how to disarm mines with Corporal Pajanias. The ammunition officer, also a good friend of mine, by the name of Malczakowski, had stashed seven mines which had been dug up, and the ammunition officer requested permission to explode them so that they would no longer be harmful. So this Corporal Pajanias and the padre, without authorization, decided they were going to have a look at how to disarm a mine. There were three antitank mines there and, unfortunately, the one or more of them were booby trapped, and up they went. Of the Corporal we found very, very little; he was the closest to the mine. And then we found the padre and it was not a pleasant sight. So we buried our Captain Padre. It was sad; he left a mother somewhere in Poland.

After a while, we were moved again, in garrison, further south and, strangely enough, the place was called Porto Sant'Elpidio, which was only about ten miles from Sant'Elpidio a Mare where we had had our one rest during the campaign. I met some nice families there and stayed with them once or twice. One family I remember was Famiglia Pasetti, and the other Fundatto. For a couple of years after I came back from Italy I exchanged letters with them, but then I started going out to Africa, and after Africa this just petered out. Now, the Fundattos did farming and also operated a restaurant in Porto Sant'Elpidio. The pasta was very good there. It's funny, because all there was, was a little tomato sauce and a beautiful spaghetti; you mixed it up together and it was really better than any of the complicated sauces that I make.

After that I made one more trip in Italy. As my then Italian girlfriend didn't want to go on a trip, I got my driver some leave and we went together. We went through central and north-central Italy, and I had more very interesting experiences. We saw Assisi, with the St. Francis Cathedral, and its beautiful stained glass. We saw Arezzo and Perugia, which are really ancient cities, probably from about 13-1400 AD, and Arezzo was very interesting. It was a medium-sized city, about 100-150,000 people. The main street was terraced, no traffic, everyone just walked. And the place was really humming in the afternoon, after work, with all the people going up and down. The architecture was fantastic: practically every house was 500 years old. I didn't lack for enjoyment.

I visited Florence, with this beautiful cathedral, and very many treasures of art. Another city, which impressed me, and probably more than any other, was Siena. I really fell in love with Siena. They have a city square, of course, where once in a while they have horse races, right on the square. There is this beautiful Tiger cathedral, a so-called striped cathedral. Every building had a history, and you could see where such-and-such *condotierre* attacked Siena, and where they saw him, and where they fought him. That was one city, which had really organized their tourism, because it was a very, very instructive story. And there were some art treasures, particularly paintings, beautiful miniatures, and they put an explanation on every building—what was there, what were the activities, and the history—so that you could really learn the history of Siena just by walking around and reading the inscriptions.

In Porto Sant'Elpidio, we partied a little, meeting our Italian friends. We walked a lot, ate pasta, and generally relaxed as much as possible. The funny thing was, whenever we trained, it really felt like the war wasn't over, that it was still for real. Fortunately it wasn't, because much as we didn't like the Russians, I don't think we were really prepared to keep fighting.

After the Germans capitulated there were lots of vehicles, including nice cars, stashed in American depots, just held there. And everybody who had something to sell was trying to buy a car. Myself and another officer got our driver, whose name was Kapuck (and he was an awful boozer himself!), to get some liras and some cigarettes, and I think a couple bottles of booze, then sent him and one of the orderlies back to northern Italy to pick up a car. Unfortunately, on the second day of the trip, they wrecked the truck, so there was quite to do about unauthorized trips, but I think that at that time nobody was really too fussing. After all, the war was over.

CHAPTER SEVEN

BRITAIN

I applied for leave to England and somehow, through various friends, got it—six weeks. We organized a little expedition consisting of the driver, myself and another medical officer and several NCO's who wanted to get back to Germany to look for their families and relatives who had been deported for forced labor. So we got organized and bought, or rather obtained, a good supply of gas, and started out. As commander of the expedition I sat in the car with the driver all the way.

We drove through Italy and saw some beautiful old cities like Mantua, Padua and one or two others. Padua was a very, very interesting city, about thirteenth or fourteenth century, with appropriate Romanesque architecture. It was one of the seats of learning in the early Italian days, and the University of Padua was famous all over the world. I remember various Polish nobles used to send their children to Padua.

We traveled up and up and up and finally arrived at the Brenner Pass which is between Italy and Austria. There, our experience was mosquitoes. Just unbelievable. I had to pull my blanket over my head in the camp and smoked a pipe to try and get the mosquitoes off me, but it still didn't work. I was practically eaten alive.

We crossed the Brenner Pass and went down into Austria. Much as I would have loved to have seen Vienna and Graz, we didn't have time because I had to get going; my time best used helping people. So we just saw Innsbruck where we stayed one day for a rest. In Innsbruck there was a company of French female drivers, and we had a party there with a little wine and music. Beautiful, of course, Austrian alpine scenery. And on we went. Then we got into Germany.

There I saw Cologne. The Cologne Cathedral was still standing, although it was very badly damaged. There was very little in Cologne itself because there was so much damage that most people were living outside of it. They were beginning to rebuild, but it was very early in the game. We went into a couple of camps, which was all very sad; my boys never found anybody. Then we drove through the Neckar Valley, Heidelberg, and that was very beautiful. We were looking for camps all this time, but we did not find the people we were looking for. Apparently, some of these people went back to Russia before we arrived. A pretty fast evacuation.

We kept going until we reached Nijmegen, in Holland, where there had been the famous Battle of Arnhem-Nijmegen, when the British and Polish paratroopers tried to break Hitler's line and end the war early. It didn't work out; whether it was bad planning or early spying, I don't know. They were defeated, and that particular small brigade lost 345 dead. So we got to Nijmegen, and in Nijmegen we went to the headquarters in Holland and got papers to go on to England. Our group then split up. The two of us who were going to England, the two medical officers, we got on the train to Holland, and the rest returned with the truck. That was the end of the Italian campaign for me.

We started out from Holland towards the Channel, and boarded the train in Arnhem-Nijmegen, which was pretty well cleaned up after the fighting. Still, the people were not in good shape, and they looked like they could have used some more food. We got on the train and traveled through northeastern France to the Channel. It was all at night—it was a night train—so we didn't see very much. Finally the train stopped and they got us off. We had to get our luggage from some other coaches and carry it—some of it quite heavy—over to the Channel boat, and get on. For the first time I found out what they said about *le mal de mere* in the Channel was right, because an awful lot of people, not all military, were seasick, and there was rather a bad stench around.

We arrived at Dover, and after some walking around the railway tracks went on to London. There, I left my baggage in the luggage office and made a beeline for Uncle Henry, who was living in his apartment about two blocks from the DDC building at Devonshire Place. I arrived about 7:30 in the morning and started pounding on the door. They were a little surprised at that, but they opened the door and there was Henry and I meeting together in the apartment. Everybody was rather surprised because they didn't know I was coming (I think I sent them a note, but it probably didn't reach them). There was a lot of tea and talking, and some breakfast, and we kept talking some more, and then, after a while, we went out to the late Matters, Uncle Leonard and Aunt Roma. We visited them at March Haddon, where I met Henry Moore, who was a great friend of Leonard's, and we had a very good time. I also met Aunt Tuna and Aunt Edda, who were living together there, and Richard. Richard was gradually deteriorating as a result of Wilson's disease, and eventually he needed full-time care. And I heard the sad news that very many of my relatives were dead, including my mother and sister, and others; generally, there had been an awful slaughter.

After a day or two, I took off for Edinburgh to find out what was going on in British medicine, and to see some old friends. What I discovered was that some of them were still working in Edinburgh, working in the same hospital, and apparently fairly comfortably off, although not much money. We had a little chat, but we were on completely different wavelengths. They lived, doing productive work, but so normal. Three meals a day and a tea break, so many hours with the patients and the odd emergency, go to a show and go to bed. Our lives were completely different. Really, we didn't have too much to talk about. Funny how things change.

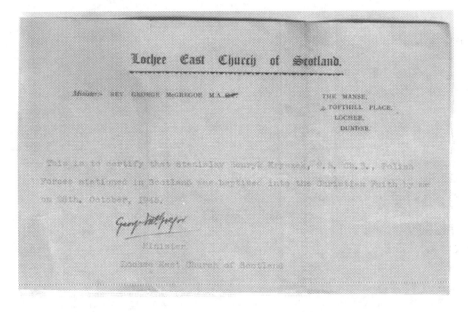

Baptismal Certificate, 1945

At that time there rose the possibility, though remote, of marriage, but it didn't pan out. After a while, in Edinburgh we had a big parade, a victory parade. The war was ended, Japan finally capitulated, and on the parade there was the worst rainfall I ever saw. World War II ended in May of 1945. Twenty million soldiers killed, and thirteen million civilians dead.

The next thing that happened, I got a chest pain, and then I got pneumonia. So I went to my old hospital and they kept me there for a week, giving me sulfur, and I got better and left. But I got six weeks' sick leave, because apparently quite a large part of my lung was involved. I got on the train and went back to London, and then out to March Haddon where I stayed for about ten days with the Matters. Leonard was still working at that time, he was a Labour MP, and afterwards a journalist. He came from Australia, but he never went back, except for one visit. They had a great big cat, Jerry, that was extremely intelligent, and could spread the table and eat his dinner. He was also fairly adept at catching rabbits.

Then I decided to go back to Edinburgh. I spent a night or two with Uncle Henry, then got on the train again and took off for Edinburgh, where I stayed until the end of my sick leave. I saw a few shows, a concert or two, but money was short and food was short. I had one of my friends, who was with me in Italy, married to the owner of a restaurant, a very nice lady. The butcher who was supplying the restaurant used to let us in at night, and let us have a little extra meat to take and cook. His name was Jimmy.

After all this time, they then wanted to send me back to Italy. I was, in fact, quite prepared to go, but the powers that be said I should go, for the time being again, and be attached to the base depot. Those base depots haunted my life right through the war! First, I went back down to the Matters' for a couple more days. Leonard wasn't so well, and I wanted to spend time with him. I saw Uncle Henry, and really, that was a nice break. I met a few other Polish people from that area, amongst others a man by the name of Marion Hammer, who was one of the best Polish poets.

And then I decided to go back to Edinburgh again. Fortunately, I had a rail pass, so I got on the train and it was the Flying Scotsman, from King's Cross to Edinburgh, and that's how I met the woman I married, Monica Margaret Renner. She was the oldest of three children, with a younger sister and brother, and her birth-date was December, 1919.

We were in the third class carriages, which were quite comfortable, though well-packed, and there weren't too many people. It was Christmas, 1945, and there was an old lady travelling to Scotland to see her great-grandchildren. She opened up a big box of goodies and had her tea, but she was a little feeble, so we sat across from her, Monica and I, and helped her. After she had her dinner, and we had a few cookies with her, we decided to go out and have a cigarette and just look at the train. We talked about how the Flying Scotsman was a beautiful train, even in those days, and we just sat there and talked, and we were kind of getting a bit friendly, and one thing and another, and we decided to meet again the next day, which was Sunday.

We went out to have a drink and it was rather amusing because, with the Scottish drinking laws as they were then, I could drink but Monica couldn't because she was not a resident of the hotel, she was just a visitor. So I had to get a drink, pour it into a little glass, and about ten minutes later order another one for myself again, and that way we kept one drink going between the two of us. We spent some nice time together, and then I went back to London.

Finally, I got a new posting. I was to be a medical officer in the reserve unit in Montrose, Scotland. I was travelling back and forth between Montrose and Edinburgh to see Monica, who was working as a resident obstetrician in King's Common in England. We managed to meet one way or another, and one thing led to another, and we got engaged. About the same time I met Audrey, Monica's sister, and Chippy, who had become good friends and were courting, and it wasn't long before we all got married.

TO WHOM IT MAY CONCERN.
—————————————————

It is to certify that Lieutenant STANISLAW HENRYK KRYSZEK, Polish Army Medical Corps, obtained permission from G.O.C. 1st Polish Corps to marry Dr Monica Margaret RENNER, of Edinburgh, on the 22 August 1946.

This is to support the original certificate written in Polish.

Grandshaft Barracks,
Dover.
15 Aug 46.

Capt.R.A.
66 Transit Camp.

Marriage Announcement and Marriage Permission

***Left to right: Aunt Edda Kryszek, Uncle Henry Kryszek, Stanley,
Monica, Unknown, Annetta (McLay) Renner, Audrey (Renner) Steer***

DISTRICT .... HAYMARKET

DISTRICT .... EDINBURGH

CITY of EDINBURGH

Extract of Register of Marriage, 1946

Monica and I were married at the Church of the Good Shepherd in Edinburgh, which was an Episcopal Church, and we were married by Monica's father, an Anglican priest. It was all very modest, being post war, and great austerity. However, we had some wine, and a good wedding cake cut with a sword; Chippy, a major in the regular forces, supplied his sword. It was August, 1945. For our honeymoon, we went to a place in the Hebrides. It was a little island, and it had a very nice hotel, nothing fancy, but the food was good and the people were pleasant, and they had Scottish dancing three times a week, which Monica loved. After the honeymoon, I went back to the hospital.

Monica had finished her residency and I was still in the army, so we went to live in a place called Whitchurch, in Shropshire, which is on the West Border, not too far from Rexham. We rented a large sitting room, with availability of bath and kitchen, and we lived there while I took a commuter bus to the hospital every morning and night.

One day the order came out that medical officers with so many months or years of active duty could go and work in a hospital for so long. I got to the hospital, which was No. 4 Polish General Hospital in Shropshire, and started working, but within three days I was sent to Dover to receive transports of displaced persons from across the Channel. And there was my medical training being wasted. I just sat on the train, drove to Dover, had a drink and breakfast in the officers' mess, and back to the seasickness of the poor DP's.

That went on for a while. Your mother, in the meantime, was sitting in her room in Salop, waiting for me to get another posting. I was then sent and put in charge of a camp, which was also for displaced persons, at a little disused airport, a little aerodrome. I got there, and that was really limit, the end of the world. It was in Wales. Very nice and very good farm breakfasts, but as they say, *Wig Wiezdow* (pronounced "Vig Veezdoff")—nothing but the wind whistles through it. And there was my wife sitting around back in Shropshire, so I got on the train and went to see the colonel medical boss. Unfortunately, I got into a disagreement with him.

The boss didn't want to see me because I didn't have an order to go and see him, so I told him, "Look, I'm paying for this." Well now, I got two weeks' CB, which means Confined to Barracks, and I was sent back to the old camp where I had initially started in the hospital. Now, officers in confinement are supposed to have everything supplied in their quarters, but somebody forgot, and they didn't give me anything to eat for about twenty-four hours. I had arranged with a friend of mine to smuggle me some food through the hole in the door, so I wasn't really hungry, but I started calling for help, and when the guardroom people came to find what was going on, I said I had hunger pains because I had not been fed for two days. There was a terrific to-do, and while I wasn't given any relief, I was given food.

That particular commanding officer in the hospital was a terrible twit. He said he had orders to punish me, so I said, "What the hell is this; this is another issue. There doesn't seem any point in having all this inquiry and all this discussion; if you have the orders to punish me, go ahead, punish!" And he did.

They let me out eventually, but in the meantime there was a lot of talk about that particular incident! One of the older air force officers with us kept telling the commanding officer "The *Daily Worker*—which was the Communist paper in England—is only waiting until Kryszek gets out to give it to you for mistreating Allied soldiers!"

At the same time I obtained my South African visa. After having been there, and after seeing my prospects in England, I intended to move to South Africa. I wrote to the South African High Commissioner and filled out the forms, and just as I came out of confinement, after all that shemozzle, I got a South African visa. So, very snidely, I reported to the commanding officer, and requested from him demobilization, to which I was entitled, with domicile to South Africa. He nearly fell off his chair. "You can't do that! You can't do that! We need you! There may be a war!" I said "Not bloody likely!", and he let me go.

My wife was, of course, conversant with all these details. In the meantime, with all these troubles, she had started working in Liverpool as an obstetrician. I took off for my demobilization, and got on the train and traveled to Land's End, to a place called Truro, which is the farthest stop on the line in the snowy wastes of Land's End. That was in November, and it was really snowy. I reported there at 10 o'clock in the morning, and by 12:30 I was demobilized. One of my friends drove me in his car to catch the train, which had in the meantime left from Truro to Wick, but he caught it at Wick, and I got on. I learned that it was long, long train ride to Scotland. I arrived in Glasgow, and went to the demobilization depot, where I was given a civilian suit, a hat and a coat, and so on. The clothes weren't very good, but they were civilian.

I headed back from Glasgow, and went straight to Liverpool, to Monica, who was pregnant with our child. We had to apply for her visa and get separate transportation, as we weren't able to travel together. I couldn't take my wife because there was a waiting list, and she had to wait behind for a while. There were so many millions of people trying to get home, or be repatriated or demobilized, that there was no way for any regular setup. Eventually, I got a notice from the Blue Funnel Line, about two or three weeks later, that there was a passage for me. I rushed down to London to say good-bye to everybody, and went to Liverpool, where the boat was sailing from. I said good-bye to Monica, leaving her behind to follow, and I was sent to Durban, South Africa, first class—at the King's expense.

CHAPTER EIGHT

SOUTH AFRICA

The boat to South Africa was a civilian boat, although it was still under military regulations, and there was no way to get private cabins or anything like that. I was supposed to be in a first-class cabin, but the one-birth cabin had been converted into four, with four bunks. So, on I got, and out we started. It was a very slow boat, only going about 11 knots an hour.

The ship, the good ship *Nestor*, was about 35 years old, and this was to be its last planned voyage. Even though the ship was so slow, the journey, as far as possible, was thoroughly enjoyable. I saw the south seas again; the Southern Cross, flying fishes, whales and porpoises, and birds, particularly a bird which the South Africans call "mollymock", which is a variety of albatross. There were a lot of very interesting people aboard, such as Lord Matthews, who created the Austin Morris automobile factories and established many charitable, particularly medical, foundations; Mr. Hanks, his managing director; General Freddie De Guingand, who was Chief of Staff to Field Marshal Montgomery; and several other people.

The journey as far as Cape Town took about twenty-two days, as opposed to fourteen to fifteen days with a fast mail boat. I didn't mind because it was a very, very nice relaxation. I had finally got my long-awaited vacation, even though it was quite crowded. In my cabin there was a young South African by the name of Archer, who was seventeen and married to a girl of twenty-one. There were four men, and four women in the dormitory and, of course, with the situation, there was no such a thing as couples. So we organized our cabins so that Archer could see his wife once in a while, and we all got out.

In addition to Archer there was a Sir William Morris. He was a schoolmaster from Pretoria, and the funny thing about him was that, with the unforgiving temperatures, he was afraid of neuralgia. Of course, we kept all the portholes open because it was terribly hot and humid. We'd all go to bed and after a while, suddenly, the temperature would become absolutely stifling and oppressive; Sir William Morris had closed the porthole. With four people in eight square feet of space you can just imagine what that created without air conditioning (we had ventilation, but no air conditioning)! Eventually I spent some of my time on deck, because at least there it was cooler.

Salt-water soap was sold in the ship's pantry, and we bathed in salt water with mugs of fresh water for rinsing off. Still, we managed to survive it all. There was a fair social life—we had a fancy-dress party—and played various games like housy-housy and twenty questions.

Finally we arrived in Cape Town, where we moored for a couple of days at the coaling wharf, and I went to see some friends that my cousin Waldi had introduced me to in Cape Town, but they were away. However, I had a tram ride through a section of the Cape, and it was very, very pretty. South Africa is a beautiful country. Then I got back to the ship, which, being a collier, was all sooty, and two days later went back and reboarded with some other passengers and cargo, and went on to Durban, which was my destination.

Durban was also a very pretty city. I got a great welcome there because they were looking for prominent visitors, and I became a prominent visitor. Our photographs even appeared in the newspaper. I stayed in the Mayfair Hotel on the top floor, the eleventh floor. The funniest thing was, I went to have a bath and, in the bathtub, there was a little line of black ants marching out, one by one. But Durban was really very nice.

Newspaper clipping, Stanley's arrival in Durban, 1946

I didn't have very much money at all, and couldn't possibly afford to stay at the hotel for any length of time, so I found a place a little less affluent. I found a smaller place, and after a couple of days in Durban, which was a very, very friendly city (that's where I saw my first Zulu), I got on the train, and I went from Durban to Johannesburg. I saw the so-called Karroo, which is South African bush, and saw the so-called *kopjes*, little hills, and then I got to Johannesburg, which was a different kind of city again, a modern, bustling, American-type city.

There I got in touch with some friends, who used to be in the British air force and had come to South Africa to try and start an import-export business, and put up with them in a modest hotel—the Sterling Hotel—and I sat there trying to get my registration, find a job, and so on. Things weren't going very well. I filled some forms in Johannesburg, and then I went to Pretoria, which was rather a beautiful, monumental city. In Pretoria, I filled more forms, and I waited. I went back to Johannesburg, to that hotel, and I sat there, unhappily wasting time.

The two airmen and I bought a car, a fairly ancient car, seven to ten years old, but in very good shape; it was an old-time Ford V-8. Most of the cars in South Africa were American; that is, they were assembled in South Africa, in the same way as is now done in Canada. We drove around; made a few short friends. In one place we rescued a middle-aged couple whose car had broken down, and they had two flat tires at the same time. We fixed them up, and we wouldn't take any money, so they invited us to join them for a nice cup of tea.

I made some friends, like the Honorary Consul of Poland in South Africa, and a few other people, including an engineer who had served in my division. As well, I had the opportunity to see the heir to the Royal Family. I saw King George with the Queen, and the two princesses, Princess Elizabeth (the present Queen) and Princess Margaret, who was just a youngster. The South African Legion, and the memorable Order of Tin Hats were paraded for them, plus a lot of other organizations, both British and South African.

I still hadn't received a permit to practice medicine in South Africa when a telegram came with the news that Monica was going to travel on the big liner *Georgic*. That was great cause for jubilation, but it wasn't all that cheerful because, by that time, what little store of money I had accumulated—one person couldn't have lived on it for more than two weeks anywhere—had almost evaporated. And there I was; no license, and no job.

I returned to Durban, and awaited my wife's arrival. The ship docked, and down she came. I could see that she was very pregnant. We got together a grand reunion, we had a fine meal and, finally, got ourselves organized in one nice, big room, in the Hotel Mayfair, where we stayed for a couple of days. We wouldn't have to chase around after trains and buses to meet each other any more. Then we sat down and decided that the funds we had were not going to last very long at the Mayfair, and that we had to find a smaller place.

We started looking around and found all sorts of odd places. There was one place with a big iron bedstead, not very clean, and the lady said, "Well, that's all right. You see, the gentleman here, who is a taxi driver, he works nights, so you can sleep here at night, and he can sleep during the daytime. You can cook and everything else while he is sleeping." That didn't quite meet the requirements, and neither did several other places, so I looked at various advertisements, and there was a small hotel, about twenty, thirty rooms, with very low rates, and it was less than a block from the beach, from the waterfront. So we went there and had a look around. The place was fairly small, but it was spotlessly clean, and very friendly, and it would do us for a little while. We took it, and that was a good move, because Monica's time was getting on, and she didn't want to be rushing around.

With what little bit of food we had we settled there and waited, and waited, and things were getting desperate, because the money was really going out, but no job. Then I saw an advertisement for a medical officer for Choke Timber Concessions. It was for the Bechuanaland, now Botswana, government, which was administered from its headquarters outside the territory of Bechuanaland, the so-called Imperial Reserve Mafeking, which was an extraterritorial British protectorate. There were simply no facilities to operate any kind of government, or courts, or police forces there, because all they had were a few traders and a few bushmen. At that time, there just wasn't any money in Britain to build civil service institutions there. But it was really a happy little country. I don't think it was one that was starving.

But my situation was a little drastic, so I went to the South African Legion, British Empire Service League, as an ex-serviceman. I saw the executive secretary, and applied for a loan. I said that I had a job in view, here is the advertisement, here is my interview recommendation, but I just don't have the money. Those people, the South African Legion, lent me the money, interest-free. Of course, I joined the Legion, which was only fair.

I got the loan, and Monica and I looked over the form and decided that I would go on to Mafeking to apply for the job. I set off on the train from Durban and after some few hundred miles (more like 1500 miles), and having traveled through Pietermaritzburg, which was the capital of Natal and a very beautiful city, clean and decorative, I arrived in Mafeking at the crack of dawn. During the Relief of Mafeking in the South African War, it was thought that here was going to be this great big fortress, but it was more like a little city square, a small one, and nothing else. This was the whole town, mostly new houses, with the population of 3,000 living on the outside. I walked around, until it was time to report for my medical.

I reported, had an interview, and then a medical. I had a little medical trouble, some protein in my urine, a minimal amount. We decided that, as I never had any kidney problems, it was probably just from sitting for hours in the train. He said, "You'd better drink some water or juice and come back." So I walked up and down, drank some water and juice, came back, and then he did the specimen and said, "Hell, that's all water! You drank so much, that's practically all there is!" But he said that's all right, that means there can't be anything serious, and I passed my medical. We talked, and he asked me all about my history, and training, and military service, and he asked me about Monica, and I got the job. That doctor, Dave MacKenzie, who was quite fond of Scots and Scotland, and who was director of the medical services for Bechuanaland, got me into the game.

I traveled back much more happily than I had traveled out because, even if it wasn't a great big job, it was a modest living, and starvation wasn't looking us in the face anymore. From then on I was allowed to draw some allowance until my regular salary came in, so off we started from our little hotel, and traveled from Durban to Bulawayo. We arrived in Bulawayo and settled, and decided that under the circumstances, seeing that I was going to real, primitive, bush, and Monica was due in only two months, she would stay in Bulawayo, and I'd just rush back and forth when the time came. I would be in northern Bechuanaland, at the other end, and the Imperial Service was at the southern end of the country, so it was really confusing.

Anyway, I got Monica settled, it was only a hotel, and I started out for my job, because I just had to go and start working and start making some money. I arrived in Victoria Falls, which was the nearest railway station to Bechuanaland, and the manager of the mill met me, a very friendly, gruff, heavy man by the name of Harvey—very rough, a kind of rough diamond. Then we went to the Victoria Falls Hotel where, for something like three and sixpence, we had a sumptuous lunch, and I was shown the outside of the Falls, because we didn't have the time to make a detailed tour, but it was still extremely impressive. In fact, I could see the Falls even from the train, coming in; there was so much spray, it could be seen it for miles.

Out we started for Bechuanaland, some five hours' drive through bush and karroo. I saw my first close glimpses of game in its natural habitat. We stopped at the general store in Victoria Falls, and got a few supplies, and then we drove in a Ford car belonging to the lumber company in Serondela, which was the name of the place across the border from Rhodesia into Bechuanaland. We traveled across Mapanifle, which was full of antelope, ostrich and other game, as well, particularly birds. We arrived in the evening, and I was given a fairly hearty dinner, a bath and a bed. Next morning, I met everybody, people with colorful names like Bookie Berger, Buddy Buddenhorst, Don de Bochlen. Some of them had their wives and families there. I could not say that they were either educationally or politically educated, however, they were good people and stuck together.

Then I saw my bush clinic, which was a kind of barrack, fortunately with doors and windows, some beds and a hospital assistant by the name of Ian Dalton Robertson Mohwela. He was one of the blackest individuals that I have ever seen. His name, Ian Dalton Robertson, was obviously a result of having worked with a missionary by the name of Robertson. I looked at the few patients; then I went to the mill, which was still in a stage of construction. There were some operating machines, but a big boiler, which was operated by gas heated with wood, was still under construction. I met the engineer there, by the name of Joe Bunche, and we got quite friendly. He was working on this big machine, and apparently, there was some second-hand equipment there, and he had a terrible job trying to fix it up.

I looked around the bush, and looked at the woods. It was mostly hardwood stands. The wood was called *mukusi*, and it was Rhodesian teak. It was very hard wood. There was no way you could chop it, and it had to be cut with special saws. The product made there was parquet flooring. Those parquet tiles were put on 10-ton Leyland trucks, and driven through the bush to Rhodesia Falls, to be exported. The Leyland trucks were British-made, and very good, but nothing really could stand up driving in that bush for very long, so there were a lot of breakdowns.

After a while, I got settled, and Mr. Harvey said they were going to build me a house. So, one Ebele carpenter by the name of Sakala, and one assistant and two hands started building a house for me with the *mukusi* wood. They produced a house in about six days, consisting of a living room, a bedroom, and a bathroom. And it had a real bathroom, even with some running water once in a while from the mill, which otherwise had to be carried; when the mill wasn't operating, we had to carry our water. Then we had our "pickaninny *kaya*"—a little house—which was a very unusual contraption, the outhouse, and the whole thing was built on rock, so they had to blast it in order to dig it. That done, we had a little two-room house on stilts with a bath. There was an adjoining kitchen, where the servants had their rooms, and a pantry, which was a real paradise for mice, and the local cats had a field day trying to protect our food.

I began to get used to the fact that you could hear leopard cries and baboon cries right around the place. The district was an elephant reserve, with some 400 elephants in it, and once in a while there was a great big mess, when an elephant decided to leave his visiting card. There were a lot of baboons and, unfortunately, there were also a lot of scorpions, which weren't such a healthy form of wildlife. There were wildcats; there were occasionally lions; there were a lot of antelope, particularly wildebeest, or gnu, and bushback. The most magnificent of them all was the eland, which was almost the size of a bull, only a little taller; kudu, with long spiral horns; waterbuck; impala. There where some rhinos, but not in our area; they were a little further west, in Ngamiland. And there were a lot of snakes of all kinds; some of them were rather dangerous.

After the house was built, and everything got organized, I went back to Bulawayo, and looked in on Monica, and everything seemed all right. I spent the weekend, and I went back to the bush. Then I got notice from her that things were starting to happen, so I rushed to the truck, and went back on the train, and I arrived in Bulawayo again. I went to the hotel, and I was told that Monica was in hospital. I rushed to the hospital—it was the Levy-Rodwell Maternity Home—and Monica was there, but she wasn't feeling terribly well, and the going was a little hard. I talked to Dr. Joe Barron, who was the obstetrician, and he said that things were all right; it would take a little while, but they wouldn't have to use any surgery. She would be all right. The delivery lasted another day and half, and eventually I was told that I could come and see my daughter, and I went, and she was with her mom, and I was very happy. I stayed for a day, then I went back to work overnight, and distributed a few cigars.

Jean and Monica, 8 August, 1947

Stanley, Jean and Monica, 14 September, 1947

As soon as I knew Monica and the baby—we named Jean Marie—were ready to come home, I took off and brought them back to Bechuanaland. That little house turned out to be quite useful; we probably had a little more space than a small apartment. Mind you, it was all wood, and not too much fuss, and in the kitchen was an old stove. We had a chicken coop, and a chicken house, which occasionally was raided by wildcats and leopards. But it was fairly pleasant.

One problem was the lack of fresh food, because the only thing, at that time, that the Africans farmed for was corn; we used to call it "mealies". Cassava wasn't terribly nutritious, and all the other food was imported. Our laborers were receiving two pounds of corn a day, and two pounds of meat a week, when supplies held or when it was imported. Because there was very little fresh meat, I was entitled to shoot for the pot after twenty-four hours away from the station. The reason being that the bearers and the laborers had to be fed, and the meat wouldn't keep. So the meat had to be eaten, and a fresh batch brought in. In fact, we only had fresh meat three or four times in more than a year. There were cattle ranges in Ngamiland, run by Cypriots. But that was a long trek. Lions took a lot of cattle, and they were being exported to Rhodesia anyway. But whenever some cattle were ranched through, we used to get one beast slaughtered, and then buy whatever we could. On one occasion, we even bought a leg of lamb. The trouble with that particular lamb was that it was an awfully fat old ram, and I had no idea how that thing ever walked, because there were just tiny little strands of muscle tissue, and the rest was pure fat. We served it up, it was the only thing we had, and one of the bosses, who was visiting, said, "Oh, I love lamb fat", but I think he had the biggest indigestion of his life the next morning! We also, once in a while, used to get, as they say, a nice fat goat. The only other thing we could get, and that was very, very seldom, was an odd chicken. Some of the Africans were willing to sell small, scrawny chickens at a good price, which I didn't mind paying, because there was nothing else.

But we lived on cans, formula and such, because, strangely enough, the baby was safer using formula, prepared properly, and sterilized, than attempting to breast feed in a place like that. However, even then, Monica nursed Jean for three months, full time, and then another three months half time, so she got a little mother's milk in her life.

Life was rather pleasant. The women got along together rather nicely. Monica's educational standard was probably 200% above every other of the Chobe ladies. She seems to have adjusted very well, and everybody was very friendly. However, there was a problem. After a few months, the baby started getting sick more and more, mostly diarrhea. We decided that, until Jean was bigger and stronger, we would have to part again. It was a very sad thing, but we decided that mother and daughter would have to go back to Bulawayo and get a decent place, a decent apartment, and see what happens next.

I took Monica around a little bit before she left, so she could see a hippo pool and a lot of the game. Of course, anywhere we traveled, game was right there, often right in the compound. Unfortunately, so were the snakes. On one occasion, Jean was in her perambulator, and a snake—a poisonous boomslang—was all curled up on the windowsill in front of her. One of the fellows in the mill, his name was Joe Uppenshaw, came in (the young fellows very often used to come in; they didn't have wives, they didn't have any social life, so they'd come and visit the family home) and when Joe saw the snake very close to Jean, he got a stick and snuck up and struck the snake.

We returned back to Bulawayo and found a nice three-room apartment to set up Mummy and baby, with one nursing maid. There was a general store, and above the general store were two new apartments. The names of the owners were Mr. and Mrs. Adelski, and they were extremely friendly, and I am very grateful, wherever they are, that they were looking after Monica, because they were very, very helpful. I took off again, and that became, more or less, the story of our lives. I was about a thousand kilometers away and, unfortunately, couldn't make it very frequently, however, I managed to make three trips.

I kept working in Bechuanaland and, in time, the doctor who delivered Jean, Dr. Barron, began looking for an assistant, because his practice was growing. He was a good doctor, and Monica became his assistant, and started doing medicine again, which was quite a help because, after all, my salary wasn't that much; I started on 1,000 pounds a year, which at that time was worth about $4,000 dollars. And even with the very low cost of living in Africa in those days, that wasn't very much. I was visiting about once every one to two weeks; whenever I had the chance to catch a fast car, I got down there and spent the weekend, or the night and the day, as much as I could.

Then there was another complication. I received news from England announcing that the former Polish soldiers who were qualified in Scotland could become permanently registered as British doctors on the condition that on the 1st of January 1949, they were resident in the United Kingdom. So there was a great big kerfuffle. The little house there in Bechuanaland wasn't bad. We had quite a bit of furniture made by the local native carpenters, and your mother had a good job. But then I had to give that up, and go to England to get registered, so I resigned and packed up the same night; sold whatever I couldn't take with me to Bulawayo. I went down and stayed with my family for maybe a week. In the meantime, I went down to Cape Town again, and got a passage—not first class this time, it was tourist—and took off for England again. I remembered to send Mr. Fanning, who was the secretary of the South African Legion, the money for my loan; that I remembered.

Off I rushed back to Britain, to get my service license and complete the internship. I had to be away a whole year.

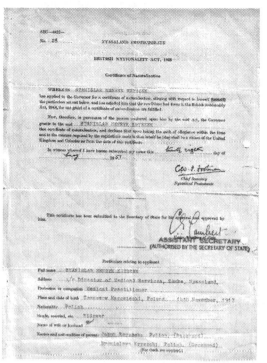
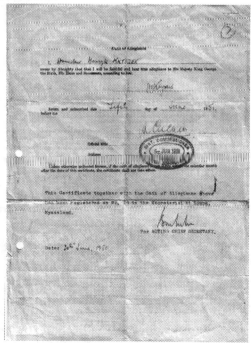

Certificate of Naturalization, 1951

CHAPTER NINE

MALAWI

Finally after getting my license and doing the residency, I came back to Bulawayo and obtained a position with the Colonial Service in a place then called Nyasaland, now Malawi. I brought Monica and Jean, who was then about three years old, and got a reasonable house, and we had some servants. The house was full of bats, but we kept it as clean as possible.

So I went to work at the hospital, a very interesting institution and medical compound, on Lake Nyasa, now called Lake Malawi. Our odd working hours were due to the climate on the lake shore which, during the early afternoon and early evening, was very hot and humid, particularly for the Europeans, who were not acclimatized to the climate there. We worked from 6:00 a.m. to 1:00 p.m., and that was it—no lunch break. I wasn't quite so fortunate, because I had to walk to the hospital for the evening hours, and there was usually somebody needing attention, after all, we had 100 to 120 patients, and some of them were quite sick. I did quite a lot of surgery, which nobody else would do, which was why I was doing it, and I don't think I killed off too many people. I treated everything from crocodile bites to malaria, bilharzia and hookworm, which were prevalent in the area.

Many patients walked in from the surrounding villages and some of them were brought in by their families. The families moved in complete with cooking pans and pots and camping gear and lived there during the patient's treatment, waiting for him to get better, which sometimes took two or three, or four weeks. So we had rather a large component there. Of course, we had organized sanitary facilities, of sorts, and we didn't have any outbreaks of infectious disease, but I was really frequently afraid of what was going to happen if something did occur. Our hospital wasn't very advanced but we had an operating room, we had beds, we had some sanitation, and the hospital started acquiring not highly trained, but very willing people. It was quite an interesting experience, and I think we did a lot of good work, particularly for children.

I saw a lot of interesting cases. I did cataract operations, a few hernias, and some other surgery as well. It was a reasonably efficient set-up. Once we had a man with about thirty or thirty-four crocodile bites. It caught him twice, and left holes all over the place. So I did some completely unorthodox things. I excised all the infected wounds and closed them up, and somehow he healed. Normally you are supposed to wait and sit until the wounds all heal, but this poor man would have been sitting there for a year if I'd done that.

I used to visit my rural dispensaries, two of them by car, and other, about a hundred kilometers away, on foot. The name of that dispensary was Mura, and it was one of my most rewarding experiences in Nyasaland, or Malawi. I only went there once a month, because it took a three days' walk each way. We had a real safari, walking through the sand, carrying bags with my chief assistants, while behind us about 26 carriers, carrying everything starting from their own food and water to the ten medical tents and the little tent in which I slept. It was quite an experience; the only time in Nyasaland when I could see a few animals, because with the rapid increase in population, the animals were already dying out there. We walked from village to village, stopping and opening our medicine boxes, and seeing the patients, and then the local headmen would come in, greet me, and I usually got a gift in the form of chicken. And then I gave them a pocketknife or half a crown in money or something like that as a reciprocal gift. And then we talked, with the usual complaints about taxes, but being a medical officer I couldn't do anything about taxes, except promise them that I would try to give them some relief. Taxes were, of course, very, very little, but then, they had very, very little, too.

Coming back from those walks, I usually felt much better from my visit to the long, distant rural dispensary. In fact, on a few occasions, I doubled the pace and walked the last two days in one. I usually found somebody to come with me; on one occasion, I had to walk alone, but there were usually one or two, either carriers or hospital aides, who wanted to go home, too.

So it went. In the afternoon, about three times a week, I saw my Chinyanja teacher, who was a schoolteacher there, and came and tried to teach me Chinyanja. I didn't learn an awful lot, I must admit; it was rather a difficult language. I used to see the chief, Chief Mesusra, who was a little fat and was an old soak, and my friend Hanishi, a Muslim, and the chief counselor of Chief Mesusra. Hanishi was a very intelligent man, and relatively well educated, by local standards. I called him my friend, and he called me his friend, and we discussed the problems of that large village, Nkhoto Kota, of 35,000 people. Hanishi used to come in about once, sometimes twice a week, and take a seat in my office, and we'd talk, and talk, about problems—health problems, and what to do with the unattached women and children, and what to do about the food situation.

My first experience in Nyasaland was famine. I arrived in Nyasaland just as famine was in full swing. The crops had completely failed, and if it weren't for the maize from the Argentine, which the British government brought all the way up to Malawi, there would have been an awful lot of death. and there was some. We walked through the villages looking for malnutrition, and we carried a scale, and we weighed everybody. It was a very crude method, but the only one feasible under the circumstances. If the average weight was over 114 lb., that village was considered to be not requiring major aid. If it was below 114 lb., they all received a ration of food, which was repeated daily. Hanishi was very helpful with this survey, and Chief Mesusra was also supportive, but he was drunk so frequently, that he wasn't much help. In the early days, after we arrived, there was *njaba*, the native name for famine, but somehow the mortality wasn't significant, and the system must have worked, because the most needy ones got something to eat.

That was an experience, the experience of hunger. In fact, I remember a tin plate I bought from which I ate mostly rice, because there was a rice company there, and I got enough rice to eat, and once in a while, when the trucks came in from Rhodesia, I got a can of bully beef, so I ate rice with or without bully beef three times a day. During that time, supplies were very tight on everything, because African foodstuffs were the first priority, and then there were medical supplies and such like. European foodstuffs were priority number four. The Africans hardly grew rice: they didn't like it, they preferred cassava or corn. Eventually, njaba ended, and everything returned to normal. The rice cooperative was run by its manager, a German from Cyprus, Mr. Popper, with his wife, Annelie. Mr. Popper really knew what was going on in the district, because all the rice farmers worked with him, and he had an awful lot of information.

After I had been in Nkhota Kota for six to eight months, I lost my friend Hanishi. One day, he came in and said he had a little lump on his neck. I examined him and I found a lot of little lumps on his neck, so I sent him immediately down to Rhodesia, because I thought that he had Hodgkin's disease. That, unfortunately, was confirmed, and Hanishi underwent radiotherapy in a Rhodesian hospital. Unfortunately, in those days, there was no other treatment; now, there are some other methods of treatment, and life can be prolonged. However, he did get better after he went through radiotherapy, and he came back, very thin and still active, and we had many more good talks, planning for the people in the district, but it wasn't long before he died. It was very sad, because he was my best friend in Africa, and it was a pleasure to work with him. I often wondered how that old salt Chief Mesusra did without Hanishi, who was really the one man who knew what to do about things!

This is the way it went. Once a week, maybe every two weeks, I walked to the rural dispensary, and then drove to the two other dispensaries and the hospital. Monica helped me with several operations, because she was an obstetrician, and everything was very happy. Our home was like a little farm. We had ducks and chickens and cockerels, and we had a banana grove, and we grew maize, a few pineapples, and cashew nuts, and generally made ourselves as comfortable as possible, which wasn't very easy there, but it was really not such a bad life at all. Once in a while we had earth tremors; they weren't real earthquakes, but some plaster used to come off the walls on those occasions, and the Department of Public Works would come and paint it up. Of course, we had no electricity, so we used pressure paraffin lamps. We had hot water by heating a big drum with wood, and then running it down through a pipe to the bathroom. Well, anyway, we managed to keep clean.

Our cook was good, and generally the service was thoroughly good. We had what you would call a butler, I suppose, head houseboy, who was the boss, and he hired everybody else. We paid for them, but he was his own boss. Each of them had a little apartment, usually one-and-a-half to two rooms, which were quite neat, and they were kept clean. They received food, agreed to by the chief; usually two pounds of corn a day per person, and about a pound of meat a week, and some salt. Salt was a very prized commodity amongst the Africans. Most of the poultry was growing practically wild there, multiplying, and a cup full of salt would buy a small chicken. The Mashira men looked after, amongst other things, finding supplies.

It wasn't such a bad life. We had our little farm, and the house, and Monica and Jean and I had a lot of friends coming in. The young men, who were unmarried, often visited the married couples because they didn't want to be alone all the time. One day a doctor from headquarters in Zomba, Dr. Flora MacNaughton, a fellow surgeon, came to the lakeshore for a vacation, and to see the lake. We were very happy to have a visitor, and a nice Scottish visitor at that. We enjoyed ourselves, had fun, and took her around, and out to Lilongwe. (We used to go to Lilongwe ourselves about once a month for supplies, a fast dash. Monica would say, after I had flashed past the villages, "That was a doctor, that was!") It was very pleasant until one night, we had Flora over for dinner when suddenly, Monica gave one cry, and lost consciousness. I picked her up and carried her to the bed, and she said, "Oh, I am all right," and those were her last words, she lost consciousness again and never regained it.

Dr. MacNaughton and the head nurse from the mission worked and worked; I worked too, but I was a too upset to do anything constructive, and they worked very hard. I was just praying and praying with the archdeacon. Her temperature went up and up and up, and we tried to bring it down. Flora was a good surgeon; she did a lumbar puncture, she did it twice, and unfortunately it was almost pure blood coming out. She also gave her, just in case, an antimalarial drug, and tried to give her supportive treatment. We organized a large group of natives to clear an airstrip in case we could fly her out to Rhodesia, but it was all of no avail. Her temperature kept going up, and the nurse was working, and Flora was working, trying to bring it down.

That happened at about half past ten in the evening, and Monica passed away around two o'clock. I just didn't know what hit me. We took Jean to Jimmy and Mary Johnson, the Public Works supervisor and his wife, and they looked after her, and we went back and I sat there hoping for a miracle, which never happened. I just sat, waited for the dawn, and it was the worst night of my life. Monica and I had been together barely a few months and suddenly she was dead of a brain haemorrhage. She had had a very hard life, and I didn't know much of her, really, because I was away most of the time, so it was pretty hard.

I met with the district commissioner, to make funeral arrangements, and that was that. I buried Monica in Lilongwe, over three hundred kilometers from Nkhota Kota; where there was a small European hospital. Then, I went back to Jean. I told her that her

Mummy had gone, that she would not be coming back again. She was not yet four, but she was very intelligent, and she knew what had happened. She had lost one or two little kittens, and she knew that the same thing had happened to her Mummy.

While Jean was cared for by Mr. and Mrs. Johnson, who were very, very good and kind people, I started winding up the station, because I didn't want to stay in that place any longer. About a week after, we took all the light belongings, our meager possessions, and we also took six of Jean's ducklings, because she was very fond of them, and we went to Zomba, where I became one of the medical officers in the Zomba hospital, which was the top hospital in the area. Things were very difficult. The first thing that happened was that somebody broke into the hen house and stole Jean's ducklings. That was the first time I was really mad at the Africans, because all we had were those ducklings, and they took them. That was the final indignity.

We lived in Zomba, and Iso, our so-called junior butler, had come with us and looked after Jean, and we had one servant girl there too. But Jean got sick several times within a very short space of time, and I decided it was just too chancy to stay. I couldn't just leave her on her own, without her mother or some qualified assistance, so I got in touch with Uncle Chippy and Aunt Audrey, the Steers, and we decided it would be best if she stayed with them until I finished my tour and we could be together again.

I felt really awful about Jean not being well, and not having her Mummy anymore. I had to put her on a Central African Airways Viking aircraft in Blantyre, with a ticket and a label, to Kenya, where the Steers lived. My little Jean got on the plane, and she took off, and I saw that plane getting smaller and smaller, going away and disappearing from view, and I don't think I ever felt as bad in my whole life before or after.

Jean arrived in one piece, although there was some foul-up, and the Steers couldn't find her, but the stewardess took her to her hotel, where Uncle Chippy eventually found her, and took her home, to a place called Limuru, in Nairobi. And then I was really on my own.

I worked on in Zomba, as a general duty medical officer in the hospital there. It was not a very exciting assignment, until I was assigned to a yellow fever survey. Apparently, there was a lot of yellow fever there—what they called jungle fever—which had not affected humans yet, but certain monkeys harboured the virus, and the right mosquito was present in the area. My duty was to collect a certain number of samples of blood in every area, and those samples were to be sent to Entebbe Medical Institute in Uganda for testing. There were an awful lot of suggestions that I should try to go out into the bush and shoot monkeys through the head, and collect the monkey blood. I was supposed to shoot them through the head, because that was the only way to collect enough blood. However, I wasn't such a crack shot, and I didn't feel like shooting monkeys, so that part of the survey was not done. We collected blood samples, and we looked for three kinds of mosquitoes in the water left in holes in the trees. We collected those blood samples all over the place. I collected an awful lot of blood samples from the Africans, and children also. I used to give the children a penny or a piece of candy, and the grownups generally came in voluntarily.

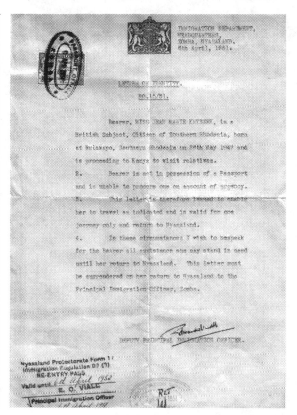

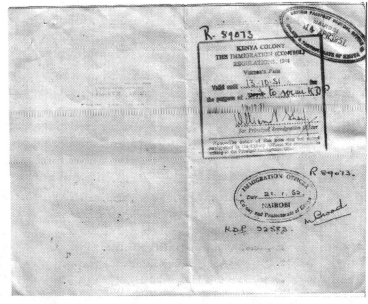

Jean's temporary travel documents, 1951

DEPARTMENT OF IMMIGRATION

Telegrams: "IMMIGRATED"
Telephone No. 4031
When replying please quote

BRANCH PASSPORT CONTROL OFFICE
ROOM 40, LAW COURTS
P.O. BOX No. 741, NAIROBI
KENYA COLONY

No. R. 89073/I.O./5.

.....19th April 1951......195....

Capt. E.A. Steer,
"A" Branch,
H.Q. E.A. Command
P.O. Box 4000
NAIROBI.

Sir,

      Please find attached hereto the Travel Document of Miss J. Kryszek who arrived at Eastleigh air port from South last saturday.

      This has been duly endorsed for her to enter as a visitor pening the issue of a Dependant's Pass to her.

      I have the honour to be,
         Sir,
      Your obedient servant,

BRANCH PASSPORT CONTROL OFFICER

WS.

That yellow fever survey took about three months of constant travel both by foot and by car, and by ferry and by boat, right from the southern border of Nyasaland to the Tanganyika border. There were some places where I was the first European ever to appear. The next thing that happened, somebody in Entebbe introduced a laboratory infection into all of the samples, and all that work went down the drain.

The survey finished at last, and I got some leave and flew to Nairobi to see Jean. I spent a very pleasant two weeks with Jean every day, and I was pleased to see that she was growing well, and she was intelligent, and getting along with her cousins. And then I went back to Nyasaland and to the end of the term of my service. During this time I met Stella Beggs Oliver, a nurse from Britain, who some years later was to become my second wife and Jean's stepmother.

After that we went to England. Jean went with the Steers, and I went from Nyasaland, and we met there when she arrived.

POST SCRIPT

I filed an application to work in Canada, and obtained it. While Jean stayed in Guernsey and in Sark, I went to Canada, by ship, by way of Newfoundland. Newfoundland didn't have a job, but Nova Scotia, my next stop, did. I started working four days after I landed, in Elmsdale, Nova Scotia. There was a doctor there, by the name of Wright, Bob Wright. Eventually, I bought a very bad practice in Brooklyn, Nova Scotia. We had some good friends, but very little money, and conditions were rather hard. I worked in Brooklyn for some fifteen months, and in January 1954, Jean joined me. Conditions were rather difficult: a lot of snow and cold, which was quite a change from the tropics. We lived, somehow, but I could not face another winter with the old broken-down sawdust furnace we had, so we moved to Windsor, Nova Scotia. We rented a small house that I later bought. It was a living, and we had very nice friends, both in Brooklyn and in Windsor.

17·9·92

Dr. Stanley H. Kryszek

Former emergency health officer dies

INDIANAPOLIS, Ind. — Stanley Henry Kryszek, MD, 84, of Indianapolis, formerly of Nova Scotia, died Aug. 26 at his home here.

A fellow of the American Occupational Medical Association, he was a physician and board member of the Harcourt Clinic, Indianapolis, until his retirement.

A native of Poland, he received his medical degree from Edinburgh University in 1941, and served in the Army Medical Corps of the Free Polish Forces during the Second World War.

After the war he became a member of the British Colonial Medical Service, and served as a medical officer in Malawi, Africa.

He resided in Nova Scotia from 1953 to 1972, practising family medicine in Windsor for several years. Later he obtained diplomas in public health and industrial health from the University of Toronto, and was appointed director of emergency health services for of Nova Scotia.

He was a lieutenant-colonel in the Royal Canadian Army Medical Corps (Militia).

He was invested as an officer in the Most Venerable Order of the Knights of St. John of Jerusalem.

He was a member of the American Medical Association, the British Medical Association, the Indiana State Medical Association, the Medical Society of Nova Scotia, and the American Industrial Hygiene Association.

He was a member of Welsford Masonic Lodge and Hiram Chapter RAM, both in Windsor.

He is survived by his wife Stella; a daughter, Jean Chard, Dartmouth; two grandchildren.

Funeral was Aug. 30 in Indianapolis.

A memorial service will be held Sept. 25 at 3 p.m. in St. Philip's Anglican Church, Halifax.

Memorial donations may be made to the Canadian Cancer Society.

Obituary

AFTERWORD

My father lived in Nova Scotia, both Windsor and Halifax, for about nineteen years. At first he was in private practice in Windsor. Later he worked for the Province of Nova Scotia as Director of Emergency Measures. He attended the University of Toronto in about 1970 to earn a Diploma of Public Health. In 1972 he and his second wife, (Stella Beggs Oliver, a British woman whom he had met in Africa after Monica's death and married in 1957) immigrated to the United States. After about a year in Harrisburg, Pennsylvania, they settled in Indianapolis, Indiana, where he was a doctor employed by the Harcourt Clinic. Diagnosed with lung cancer in 1977, he lived to see the birth of his first two grandchildren, Diana (1978) and Brendan (1981). Jacob was born in 1984, two years after Stanley died of complications of his disease. He is survived by Stella, who later married an Indianapolis lawyer, Arthur Northrup. As of this date she still lives in Indianapolis and is preparing an account of her and Stanley's life in Canada and the United States.

These memoirs were dictated into a tape recorder during the last couple of years of his life, and have been edited (from a transcript kindly supplied by Dr. Hilary Koprowski), by Richard Rudnicki, a Nova Scotia artist and writer, with some slight amendments by myself.

Jean M. Chard
Dartmouth, N.S.
March, 2006